EQUAL RIGHTS FOR ALL. SPECIAL PRIVILEGES FOR NONE

Re-Examining the Agrarian Arguments Against A Centralized American Government

Laurie Thomas Vass

The Great American Business & Economics Press
GABBY Press

First Edition Printed Copyright © 2001

Second EBook Edition Copyright © 2014

3rd Edition Printed Copyright © 2017

All rights reserved under Title 17, U.S. Code, International and Pan-American Copyright Conventions. No part of this work may be reproduced or transmitted in any form or by any means, electronic or mechanical, including photocopying, scanning, recording or duplication by any information storage or retrieval system without prior written permission from the author(s) and publisher(s), except for the inclusion of brief quotations with attribution in a review or report. Requests for reproductions or related information should be addressed to the author(s) c/o Great American Business & Economics Press, .

Printed in the United States of America
The Great American Business & Economics Press, GABBY Press

Printed First Edition ISBN: 978-0-9794388-0-6 0-9794388-0-2

Ebook Edition ISBN: 978-0-9794388-3-7

3rd Edition Printed ISBN 978-0-9794388-8-2 0-9794388-8-8

TABLE OF CONTENTS

Introduction: The Anti-Federalist/Agrarian Arguments Against Centralization — 4

Chapter 1. What Lessons of History Did The Agrarians Teach About Creating A Natural Rights Free Society? — 17

Chapter 2. The Agrarians Arguments Against Unfair Constitutional Rules of Procedure — 59

Chapter 3. The Agrarian Interpretation of Individual Morality In an Individualistic Equal Rights Society — 66

Chapter 4. Rational Choice in An Individualistic Decentralized American Government — 77

Chapter 5. The Rationale of the Federalist Centralization of Government Power — 83

BIBLIOGRAPHY — 89

Introduction: The Anti-Federalist/Agrarian Arguments Against Centralization

The phrase "Equal Rights For All. Special Privileges For None," originated in the late 1820s and captured the essence of political reforms desired by the supporters of Andrew Jackson.

Jackson's followers thought that by adopting stronger Federal government regulations of those financial interests that controlled the supply of money, that common citizens would have a better opportunity to control their own economic destiny.

One of the purposes of government, according to this line of thought, was use the power of the central government to protect the economically weak from the financially strong.

The power of the central government would provide a countervailing power to the economic power wielded by financial special interests who had organized into a political party and had used their political power to control the supply of money, through their control of the central bank.

Those who opposed Jackson also had their own philosophy of government, which highlighted the benefits of the free market as complementary component to the political system.

In their view, a strong national bank would facilitate economic growth and world trade. One of the purposes of government, seen from this vantage point, is to create, and then legally protect, private economic institutions in their function of promoting the financial interests of an elite social class.

Both political factions wanted to use the power of government to accomplish different ends of society.

In both cases, as described by Larry Schweikart, in Banking In The American South From The Age Of Jackson To Reconstruction, the use of government as an instrument to achieve social ends led to increased centralized political control over the workings of the free market.

In the hands of Jackson's Democratic Party, political policy was effective in killing the bank. In the hands of the Whig Party, political power led to increased economic power, primarily used by financial institutions to enforce legal contracts involving mortgages and liens on farm property.

Either political party could have claimed historical legitimacy about the purpose of government.

TABLE OF CONTENTS

Introduction: The Anti-Federalist/Agrarian   4
Arguments Against Centralization

Chapter 1.
What Lessons of History Did The Agrarians   17
Teach About Creating A Natural Rights Free Society?

Chapter 2. The Agrarians Arguments Against   59
Unfair Constitutional Rules of Procedure

Chapter 3. The Agrarian Interpretation of Individual   66
Morality In an Individualistic Equal Rights Society

Chapter 4. Rational Choice in An Individualistic   77
Decentralized American Government

Chapter 5. The Rationale of the Federalist   83
Centralization of Government Power

BIBLIOGRAPHY   89

Introduction: The Anti-Federalist/Agrarian Arguments Against Centralization

The phrase "Equal Rights For All. Special Privileges For None," originated in the late 1820s and captured the essence of political reforms desired by the supporters of Andrew Jackson.

Jackson's followers thought that by adopting stronger Federal government regulations of those financial interests that controlled the supply of money, that common citizens would have a better opportunity to control their own economic destiny.

One of the purposes of government, according to this line of thought, was use the power of the central government to protect the economically weak from the financially strong.

The power of the central government would provide a countervailing power to the economic power wielded by financial special interests who had organized into a political party and had used their political power to control the supply of money, through their control of the central bank.

Those who opposed Jackson also had their own philosophy of government, which highlighted the benefits of the free market as complementary component to the political system.

In their view, a strong national bank would facilitate economic growth and world trade. One of the purposes of government, seen from this vantage point, is to create, and then legally protect, private economic institutions in their function of promoting the financial interests of an elite social class.

Both political factions wanted to use the power of government to accomplish different ends of society.

In both cases, as described by Larry Schweikart, in Banking In The American South From The Age Of Jackson To Reconstruction, the use of government as an instrument to achieve social ends led to increased centralized political control over the workings of the free market.

In the hands of Jackson's Democratic Party, political policy was effective in killing the bank. In the hands of the Whig Party, political power led to increased economic power, primarily used by financial institutions to enforce legal contracts involving mortgages and liens on farm property.

Either political party could have claimed historical legitimacy about the purpose of government.

The constitution is silent on the matter of how free markets promote the public purpose, and silent about the underlying relationship between the free market system and the functioning of political parties in the political system.

Because of this silence, either side could claim that their interpretation of the purpose of government was correct.

While the relationship between politics and economics served as a focal point for much of the discussion of those engaged in the making of the Constitution of 1787, the founders, and in particular, James Madison, concentrated more on developing rules of procedure than on defining the constitutional definition of the public purpose.

The rules of procedure would work well, according to Madison, if they were both created and enforced by representatives from the natural aristocracy. Madison's rules of governmental procedure tended to concentrate political power in the Federal government, and not states, but contained a system of checks and balances designed to limit despotic behavior by elected representatives at the federal level.

However, according to Madison's rules of civil procedure, the representatives had to be drawn from the ranks of the aristocracy.

In the late 1880s, an organization of American citizens, primarily farmers from the South and Southwest, recognized that the existing system of agricultural debt peonage was unfair.

Like Andrew Jackson's followers, the farmers initially focused on a series of political reforms, called the Ocala Platform, which were intended to correct the abuses they saw in both the political and economic systems.

The intent of the reforms were directed at curbing the concentration of political power exercised by financial and industrial corporations by providing for stronger Federal government regulations of market behavior.

One of the leaders of the southern agrarian movement, Tom Watson, of Georgia, revived the phrase "Equal Rights For All. Special Privileges For None," and placed it in the masthead of his newspaper.

In this later historical setting, the main target of reform was the repeal of legislation which deployed the resources of government to enforce the debt-peonage contracts that were causing farmers to lose ownership of their farm lands.

The manner of operation of the financial rules made it impossible for common citizens to ever get out of debt.

By the early 1890s, the leaders of the agrarian revolt had come to the conclusion that the whole constitutional framework of making and enforcing the laws were rigged against the interests of common citizens.

Madison's carefully devised system of constitutional rules had succeeded too well in insulating the influence of the common citizens on the workings of the political system.

Once in place, this system of insulation provided no remedy for the citizens to reassert control over the special interest manipulation that Madison's rules of procedure had created.

As Gordon Wood has pointed out, in The Creation of the American Republic, not only did Madison's scheme provide for a system dominated by "...natural leaders who knew better than the people as a whole what was good for society," but it also succeeded in removing the non-natural leaders from the political process.

Wood noted that "In fact, the people did not actually participate in government any more...The American (Federalists) had taken the people out of the government altogether.

The true distinction of the American government wrote Madison in the Federalist #71 'lies in the total exclusion of the people, in their collective capacity, from any share in the government.'"

The agrarians thought the root of their financial problems was special interest manipulation by the elites in political rule making and law enforcement. The solution to the problem, they thought, was a new type of political cooperation that featured equal rights and equal opportunity as the end goal of the political system.

Part of the agrarian's political strategy was to operate a massive, national educational campaign, designed to educate common citizens about the unfair rules.

Part of their strategy was to create new forms of financial cooperatives that led to a cooperative economic effort on farm supply buying and produce marketing.

After the initial efforts at political reform within the existing system had failed, the farmers concluded that reforms that relied solely on increasing the centralized power of government through new regulations of special interests would not be enough to solve their problems.

They also concluded that neither of the two major political parties could be the vehicle for their reforms.

Madison's natural aristocracy had captured and controlled the internal workings of each party, and also controlled, through patronage, the agencies of government.

This dual position of power, over both the political parties and the agencies of government, allowed the special interests to effectively shut off or control the direction of regulatory reforms sought by the agrarians.

The discovery by the agrarians that the elites dominated both political parties was not a new topic in American history.

The framers of the Constitution had discussed this topic at length, during the ratification debates of 1788.

John Adams wrote about it in his book, Thoughts on Government, and devoted considerable attention to the problem of how Madison's rules would lead to a "system that rewarded, not skill and hard work, but family connections and political scheming."

Alexander Hamilton's obsession with gaining the loyalty of the wealthy to the new constitution led him, in Federalist #15, to conclude that "...only coercion of individuals was effective in upholding national interests."

Of course, from Hamilton's point of view, the definition of "national interests" was solely to promote the interests of the natural aristocracy.

In his review of Hamilton's work, Richard Bernstein posed the basic political question raised by the rules created by Madison and Hamilton:

> *"Was it dangerous in a democratic government, to have important officers insulated from control by the people, or was it necessary to accept that risk in order to protect fundamental rights from infringement by popular passions or political intrigue?"*

The agrarians answered the question by concluding that they had gotten the worst of all possible worlds. They had a government in the political hands of the elites who limited economic opportunity for common citizens, and who used the agencies of government to direct tax benefits to themselves.

Madison's carefully devised rules of procedure had left common citizens with no formal power to regain or reform the government.

Having reached this conclusion, the farmers broke away from the Democrat Party, in 1892, and formed the Populist, or People's Party, and adopted the phrase "Equal Rights For All. Special Privileges For None," as their political motto.

In most of the nation, the aftermath of the entrance of the Populist 3rd political party, after 1892, was the firm reestablishment of traditional two political party control over the national political structure.

However, in the South, the upshot of the Populist revolt was the successful use of the specter of "Negro Rule" by the Democratic Party to banish the Republican Party from Southern states.

In the South, primarily in North and South Carolina, the Agrarians had formed a political alliance with the Republican Party, and had succeeded in electing representatives to the legislature, and to the governorship in North Carolina.

As a part of their political reforms in North Carolina, the Republicans attempted to use taxes to educate black children. The use of tax dollars to educate black children provided the needed propaganda for the Democrats to tar the farmers and Republicans with the epithet that the Republicans loved Negroes, better than they loved white people.

All across the South, the Democrats used a very effective term of endearment, in public gatherings, against the Republicans, about how much the Republicans loved black people.

This early use of racial fear as a political ploy by the Democrats helped to establish an enduring, one-party/white-man political monopoly, that lasted most of the twentieth century.

In the rest of the nation, the Republican Party competed with the Democratic Party within the arena of a carefully agreed upon formula. Both parties agreed that the purpose of government was to make the economic pie bigger.

The outcome of political competition, it was agreed, would be that the benefits of national government policies would be directed to whichever of the special interest groups of either party who happened to win control of Congress and the Presidency.

Real politics between the two parties relied on a cooperative political ruse that the public purpose was being served by this pseudo-political competition.

As had been handed down by Madison, the definition of the public purpose was to be determined by the elite "natural leaders."

The definition of the public purpose could vary over time, but it could be identified with the assistance of the "free press," comprised of an elite national media.

The media's contribution to political dialogue was to shape the news to fit their evolving agenda of what they thought would be good for the common folks.

National politics, within this carefully circumscribed arena, seemed to reach an equilibrium based upon, and perpetuated by, special interest cooperation among groups of elites from both parties.

For the Democrats, real politics meant the continual invocation of class war and racial injustice as a political ploy to bind blacks and the downtrodden to vote for the Democrats.

Their favorite political formula was that the rich were getting richer, poor people and minorities were victims who had grievances against the wealthy, and if Democrats were elected, these downtrodden may be able to get reparations and redress for their woes.

As in the historical case of Jackson's Democratic Party, this political formula of the modern Democrats led to increased centralized power of the Federal government over the lives of individual citizens.

For the Republicans, real politics meant that the type of Big Government policies supported by the Democrats were bad, or at least worse than the Republican type of Big Government policies.

In the hands of Republicans, the Government could hand out welfare to the favored corporations, shift the tax burden to middle class citizens, and skew national foreign policy to the interests of the emerging multi-national corporations, who in turn, favored the Republicans with political donations.

The outcome of this form of Republican politics was increased centralized power of government for the benefit of corporations and financial institutions.

While the political equilibrium offered by this pseudo-political competition fostered a period of long term stability, interrupted only occasionally by assassinations and riots, it did nothing to solve the underlying American political dilemma that gave rise in the 1830's to the first use of the phrase "Equal Rights For All. Special Privileges For None."

That dilemma boils down to finding some substitute for special interest corruption as the binding glue that holds citizens together in a democratic republic.

Following Hamilton's line of logic, if it is not elite group self-interest that creates the binding political obligations to serve the public purpose, then what other human motivation or intention is there that creates a sense of shared civic obligation?

If Madison's scheme of dispersing special interests over a vast continent did not work, then what other justification is there for a political/economic system that blocks non-elites from participation in political decisions?

One legacy of Madison's constitutional rules is that, in the absence of an explicit statement of the constitutional public purpose, the political system tends to evolve into a system of elite self-interest, and eventually into a type of special interest tyranny that subjugates individual freedom to the collective interests of the elite.

Because Madison's rules of procedure insulated the elite from the will of the citizens so effectively, the citizen's have had precious little political leverage to regain control of the system.

Through time, the American system of special interest elitism in politics has led to a condition where the social elites operate in D. C. in a nearly closed decision-making system, whose rules of participation and procedures the elites control.

As time goes on, the decisions made in Washington seem to be more and more disconnected from the consent of the citizens, and beyond the control of the citizens to participate in it, even in the most limited form of electing, every four years, the elites who will rule them.

The dilemma of finding a replacement for elite self interest in the political system is complicated by the evidence that a certain component of elite self interest seems to be exactly the right human motivation for making the free market system work.

Hamilton's concern about whether the wealthy would continue to perform their valuable function of making investments in the young economy was not misplaced.

Much of the economic experience and theory in the past 150 years has shown that the increase in social welfare in a future period depends upon keeping the flow of investment capital strong in the current period of time.

The dilemma in keeping the wealthy happy so that they will continue to make investments has become especially complicated since Adam Smith noted that the self interest of each individual in a competitive market leads to the greatest wealth in society, thus providing the logical basis for concluding that the economic self interest of elites serves the public purpose.

Madison's rules concluded that the self-interest of the wealthy was a greater good in serving the public purpose than the self-interest of common citizens to participate in a fair political system of equal rights and equal privileges.

Madison's solution to keeping the wealthy happy was to provide a mix of powers, based upon the British class system, in which the wealthy could have their very own branch of government, called the Senate, which functioned just like the House of Lords.

Further, the political rules adopted tended to keep all branches of government safely in the hands of the natural aristocracy.

As Elisha Douglass pointed out, in Rebels and Democrats, Federalist leaders, like North Carolina's Sam Johnston, understood that the problem for the new constitution was "...how to establish a check on the representatives of the people."

Few, if any of Madison's cohorts worried about the basic contradiction unleashed by their constitutional scheme.

As Douglass noted,

> "Hence, a double paradox: to preserve their own liberty, the unprivileged masses must be prevented from infringing on the privileged few; to maintain a government based on consent, a large proportion of the people must be deprived of the ability to extend or withhold consent."

As the Agrarians searched for a replacement for elite self interest as the causal agent for holding the political democracy together, they tended to rely upon a theological interpretation of how American society should operate.

Much of their rhetoric suggested that there was, or should be, a divine relationship in directing the affairs of the nation. God's divine guidance was not a new interpretation of the American condition.

Michael Zuckert, in The Natural Rights Republic, identifies the covenant theology of the Puritans as one of the three sub-themes to the dominant tradition of natural rights, which explains the origins of American political philosophy.

What was slightly different about the Populist theological message was that it was not based upon the God of Faith and Revelation in a secularized covenant, as in the Puritan's interpretation.

The Populist interpretation was based upon a God who had equal love for every individual, which led the Agrarians to a natural rights conclusion of moral and political equality.

The Populist interpretation of God relied upon a faith that each individual had an equal ability to grasp self-truth and the truth of equal natural rights because man resembles God in terms of dominion.

The dominion of God in Heaven, according to the Agrarians, was the same kind of thing as man's dominion on earth. God admitted man to share in His dominion as a starting point in human history.

This natural rights orientation to God's relationship to American society was explored by Richard Tuck, in Natural Rights Theories: Their Origins and Development.

Tuck describes the relationship as one of reciprocity. Tuck wrote "...by using his intellectual and spiritual resources, and with sacramental grace, man could come to be the same kind of being as God...the relationship between God and man as a reciprocal one between equals...which generated rights on both sides."

It was this interpretation of the reciprocal relationship between God and man that resulted in the massive educational ventures of the Agrarians to educate common farmers about the American political and economic dilemmas confronting the farmers.

The Agrarians believed that if they showed the citizens the truth of their theological propositions, as those propositions applied to political reform, that the citizens would act upon the truth.

It was not the specific outcome of a political question that mattered so much to the Agrarians, but the open process of evolution, and the freedom to evolve, that concerned them.

God's relationship with man was dynamic and evolving, and involved an on-going reciprocity. The Agrarians applied the logical connection between the theologically derived search for self-truth and the establishment of constitutionally fair rules of cooperation in a natural rights republic that would allow for the determination of political truth.

The Populist's emphasis on individual equality in rule making and political rights came from their theology of commonality and social equality that southern non-elites felt towards each other, no matter what the social or economic status of the other.

In his book, Common Whites: Class and Culture In Antebellum North Carolina, Bill Cecil-Fronsman quotes an observer traveling through the South in the early 1800's.

The observer remarked that common whites, in North Carolina, were "...extremely tenacious of the rights and liberties of republicanism. They consider themselves on equal footing with the best people in the country, and upon the principles of equality, they intrude themselves into every company."

The feelings of social and political equality of common people arose from the priority they attached to attaining self-respect and economic independence.

They believed that their own moral worth as individuals did not derive either from their initial endowment of labor, or from their accumulation of property from market transactions.

Their moral worth was granted to them by a God who loved each individual.

According to this historical interpretation, what the common whites in the South were attempting to establish, in contrast to what the plantation elite actually established, was a commonwealth of independent producers, far removed from the sphere of power generated by the plantation aristocracy.

Thomas Jefferson captured the essence of this philosophy in many of his writings, and in two of his witty sayings.

In the political realm, Jefferson suggested that the goal should be a civil society "where no man should do against his will the bidding of another."

In the economic realm, Jefferson advocated a society "where no man was so poor as to be forced to sell himself, and none so rich as to be able to buy him."

Within the first five years of their existence, the Agrarians had analyzed the American political and economic system, and had shifted their emphasis from regulatory and political reform to constitutional reform.

They were in the early stages of defining a replacement for Madison's reliance upon the natural aristocracy. Before they could implement their ideas, they were engulfed in the political counter-attack of elites from the two dominant political parties.

The purpose of this book is to start over in American history, at the point of the anti-federalist arguments, and re-examine the Populist's legacy of fair political participation, and to explore the question of the relationship between the pursuit of individual self interest, free market economics, and the constitutional public purpose.

The book's main argument is that the adoption of the anti-federalist/agrarian arguments against centralized government would have been a better pathway to preserve individual freedom than Madison's constitutional rules of procedure.

In making the claim that the current constitutional system is beyond redemption, the book's premise is that the new natural rights constitution must empower citizens with more democracy, at the most local level of state and city government, to the end that citizens can rely on their own initiative to preserve and protect their freedoms.

The book makes the claim that the new constitution must establish the framework for voluntary agreements to be made and enforced in morally binding obligations to follow civil rules in a free society.

Obligation to serve the public purpose in the anti-federalist populist heritage derives from the recognition of reciprocal advantage to achieving individual independence obtained from social cooperation in civil rule making and rule enforcement.

Each individual is assumed to have a biological capacity to see Jefferson's self evident truth of the reciprocal advantage to be gained through voluntary cooperation. The reciprocity in this system of political authority is based upon an exchange of trust that others will honor the claims and rights of others.

The bedrock assumption in this natural rights constitution is adherence to the rule of law.

The anti-federalist argument was that political rights are not distributed according to economic power or property ownership, but through political exchanges between citizens that reciprocity will be honored.

A citizen in this type of constitutional democracy continually goes through the mental process of gauging what level of trust to exchange with other citizens by this calculation:

> "I'll vote for rules that make you happy and free because I can "imagine" that I may end up on the bottom of the totem-pole of rights, and become disadvantaged by the adoption of these rules."

The rules of political cooperation developed through the process of reciprocal exchange of trust continually bind the individual to the system of authority because the individual can imagine that political rules and rights could easily be reversed, or worse yet, be dictated by a self-interested political elite.

The social glue that holds dissociated individuals together in this political system is the recognition by each individual that the advantages gained through politically equal cooperation for each individual are greater than the costs derived from unequal individual freedom.

By imagining the sovereignty of another as if it were the individual's own sovereignty, the individual comes to the logical conclusion that the public purpose is served by cooperation in rule making and rule enforcement.

The mental ability to imagine the welfare and sovereignty of another is a biological trait provided by the evolutionary necessity of predicting the behavior of other individuals.

It is a universal human trait, and the proposition of this human trait is in direct opposition to the Federalist wisdom that only a few human brains have a superior capability to make decisions about the welfare of others in society.

The Federalist position ended up, in 2008, allowing socialists, who believe that they have a superior capacity to make decisions for every one else, to gain centralized power to impose their views on the rest of society.

Imagination, used in this context, plays the same type of role as the "state of nature" played for both Hobbes and Locke. In their case, they imagined how individuals would act in a pre-civil society, and then made some logical conclusions about the rules individuals would adopt, when they left the state of nature.

The problem with their method is that political relationships are dynamic and evolve over time. Locke's logical deductions were rooted in a static analysis of pre-civil and post-civil society based upon his analysis of an on-going social class conflict between the few and the many.

The rest of this book explores the implications of this combination of populist theology and individualistic ideology. The two key implications of the ideology are that the system of political authority of individualism must be process-based, and that the outcomes of any political exchange, and the outcome of the entire system of the natural rights republic, is always at risk and uncertain.

The extension of that trust in this system of authority, like the system of democracy itself, is an act of faith in the rationality of individual humans.

The outcomes are contingent, and what happens could easily turn out to be something else, in the absence of allegiance to the rule of law.

It is the element of decision making under uncertain conditions however that provides the key to understanding why individuals would continue to provide allegiance to the rule of law.

In Constitutional Economics, James Buchanan wrote that "Uncertainty about where one's own interest will lie in a sequence of plays or rounds will lead a rational person, from his own self-interest, to prefer rules and arrangements, or constitutions, that will seem fair, no matter what final positions he might occupy."

The two essential conditions for the new constitutional system to work are the belief that individuals pursue their rational self-interest, and that the constitution identifies the pursuit of the rational self interest as the goal of a democratic representative republic.

It did not matter how widely dispersed or balanced Madison's special interests may have been, if the constitutional public purpose of freedom and equal rights were not made as the explicit goal of his rules.

Madison's constitutional rules of procedure were a failure because they ended up, after 230 years, in the establishment of a socialist tyranny, with no civil rules of procedure to allow citizens to regain their liberties.

Chapter 1.
What Lessons of History Did The Agrarians Teach About Creating A Natural Rights Free Society?

The Agrarians of 1885 were right about the threat to citizen sovereignty posed by the huge business trusts and the consolidated power of bankers and merchants.

Before them, the followers of Jackson were right to fear the power of the National Bank as a threat to individual freedom.

Before them, Jefferson, and the anti-federalists, were correct in their assessment that Madison's constitutional arrangement would reward a favored set of special interests.

The fear of common citizens of centralized privilege, exercised in a two-party elite political special interest system, provides a great continuity in explaining American history, from 1787 to today.

About 100 years after the adoption and ratification of the new constitution, the agrarian leader, Tom Watson asked in his newspaper, "What is Labor's Fair Share?"

A better question may have been "What are Fair Rules for Labor?"

The rules of politics had been set by Madison and Hamilton to achieve separation of powers in the branches of government, the indirect election of representatives, and judicial review of legislation, all intended to bury any incipient tendencies to popular government.

In Federalist #39, Madison argued for a new sort of representative democratic republic. It would rest on the "total exclusion of the people, in their collective capacity, from any share in government."

Hamilton wrote at the time that he considered the "people as a great beast, howling masses, not fit to govern."

Madison further explained in Federalist #51 that "In framing a government of men over men, one must first empower the government to control the people, and then oblige it (the government) to control itself."

As the Agrarians discovered, the flaw in Madison's plan is that there are no citizen controls over the economic power of the political elites, and there is no way for common citizens to reform the rules through the existing two party special interest political system.

The Federalist ideology about common citizens contained an assumption that special financial interest activity would always be based upon actions that would benefit common citizens.

In their set up, the interaction of eltie commercial private interests would produce a government of common good.

What happened instead is that private special interests became group special interests, and those group interests formed political coalitions that captured the reins of a powerful central government.

Centralized political power was translated into centralized financial power, exercised to the benefit of the elites.

The common citizens in America did not benefit from this initial assumption of the Federalists that the *virtue* of the Federalists would result in a society that promoted the common wealth.

One lesson of history that the anti-federalist experience teaches is that the Federalist ideology of elite special interest, that was supposed to lead to a "common good," actually led to a collectivist group-oriented, special interest political system.

The anti-federalists were well aware of this potential outcome and tried to modify Madison's work, both before and after it had been enacted, to no avail.

In an irony of history, it was not an economic or financial interest that captured the central government, and imposed tyranny. In 2008, it was an opportunistic socialist ideology that took advantage of the Federalist flaw, and gained the levers of centralized power.

In contrast to the Federalist ideology, the Whig ideology, of 1835, began with a collectivist conception of the common good, generally derived from Rousseau's general will.

The Whigs thought that the common good was the sum of all collective social wealth, and saw individuals as a homogeneous entity in perpetual conflict with elites.

The irony is that the Whig emphasis on state and local government was much more compatible with the anti-federalist notions of individual freedoms.

What the Agrarians were searching for, 100 years later, for was a combination of the two ideologies that would feature authority by the consent of the governed, at the national level, achieved through citizen participation in government rule decision making, at the local level.

Through their efforts at economic cooperatives and mass citizen educational meetings, they came to an understanding that their individual self-interests, as farmers, could be pursued through a civil society that made the pursuit of self-interest easier to obtain.

In the mid 1880's, the farmers recognized that they were trapped in a neo-slavery debt peonage system, with no way to escape.

According to McMath, in Populist Vanguard, "Alliance leader and many farmers strongly believed the source of their problems to be the credit and marketing system of the cotton culture in which the furnishing merchant loomed as the principal villain."

As their first economic policy response, the leaders of the Alliance created a cooperative exchange network to both provide credit to farmers and market their crops.

As described by Sydney Nathans, in The Quest For Progress, the farmers soon found themselves

> "...clashing head-on with bankers, merchants, railroads and warehousemen, none eager to sacrifice their profits to the cooperative competitors...Credit and the currency supply of the entire nation, it became evident, were in the viselike grip of the county's largest bankers, who, in the name of "sound currency" had dictated two decades of deflation and tight money."

The tight money policies of the banks was financially rewarding for bond-holders, but absolutely economic death on farm prices, for farmers trying to escape debt peonage.

In addition, the tight monetary system caused a shortage of liquid cash, which was required for the payment of property taxes. Because the farmers did not have case to pay taxes, they began to lose title to their land.

The Federal monetary policy had the effect of assisting the political coalition of bankers and furnishing merchants in schemes to obtain title to the land of the small-holders.

The dual effect of taking land away from farmers was a greater concentration of land ownership, and greater number of formerly free-holders forced into the debt-peonage system.

As described by C. Vann Woodward, in Origins of The New South, "In their attack on the national banking system, the agrarian economists were on solid ground in contending that private privilege was exercising a sovereign power, a power of regulating national currency, for private gain rather than for meeting the needs of the country."

A private special financial interest exercising a sovereign political power, however, is the logical conclusion of Madison's constitutional rules of procedure.

As a second economic policy response, the Agrarians developed their sub-treasury plan, which Gavin Wright described as a system of warehouses and elevators that would accept crops from farmers and issue notes equal to 80% of the crop's values.

As a way out of the political vise grip exercised by bankers and merchants, the agrarians were trying to replace the tight money, high interest crop mortgage system of debt peonage with a plan that mortgaged the crop to the federal government at low interest.

The farmers relied upon the Democratic Party to implement their sub-treasury plan, primarily through the good offices of U. S. Senator Zeb Vance, of North Carolina.

After watching the slow progress of the sub-treasury plan in Congress, the farmers became agitated.

In July of 1890, one tenant wrote to Senator Vance, saying

> "My Dear Sir, we have been voting with the Democratic Party for the last quarter of a century looking for the relief promised from year to year by our party leaders and find none. We feel, Sir, that we have been deceived and we have become dissatisfied with those who make promises only to be broken."

As described at the beginning of this book, the two parties use the subterfuge of helping citizens overcome problems only in so far as it helps the elites in either party win elections.

The activity of the national Democratic Party in not serving the needs of farmers was mirrored by the activity of the Democratic Party at the state level.

During the late 1870s, the Populist leader, Leonidas Polk, had been successful in establishing a state agricultural agency. The state department of agriculture had been created in 1877, with Polk as its first commissioner.

It had been created with the votes of both Democrats and farm-oriented Republicans. Soon thereafter, the Democrats achieved control of the General Assembly and cut the funding for the agency, citing the high cost of operation of its 3 person staff.

Lawrence Goodwyn, in Democratic Promise, wrote that by the last of the 1880s, the agrarian leaders had seen in both political parties:

> "...abundant evidence that great aggregations of capital could cloak self interested policies in high moral purposes, and have such interpretations disseminated widely and persuasively through the nation's press, convincing the leaders of the need for a new political party free of corporate control."

The strategy of the agrarians to move into politics and to create a new political party was contentious and divisive issue, causing a split between the leadership of the agrarian movement and the farmers who had been involved with the first two efforts at policy reform.

Some historians, among them Michael Schwartz, in Radical Protest and Social Structure, believe that this underlying split between the leaders and the members of the agrarian movement explains why the Populist Party ultimately failed.

"The final option," for the leaders according to Schwartz, was a "massive entry into politics, which ultimately freed the state leadership from its dependency on membership."

The rank and file farmers had achieved economic power in the first two policy efforts, but in the new political party, the members had no power. There was no natural relationship between the farmer's role in the new party and the political changes that the political system needed to make in order to improve the lives of the farmers.

With the creation of the new political party, according to Schwartz, "The oligarchization of the Alliance had reached its logical conclusion: disembodied leadership groups appealing to a mass membership."

The irony of history is that in order to pursue the public purpose of the farmer's freedom from the debt-peonage system, the new Populist Party had to look and act like a special interest political party that appealed to farmers, as if they were just like any other special interest group.

Another important lesson taught by the agrarians is that third parties are not successful vehicles for political reform of the American special interest system.

The two dominant special interest parties are too well entrenched and will work together to kill the third party.

In their brief political life as elected leaders in North Carolina, the Agrarians were successful in implementing many elements of reform that they had previously sought through the Democratic Party.

In the Promise of the New South, Edward Ayers wrote that they

> *"established an impressive record. They rewrote the anti-democratic election laws implemented by the Democrats, set limits on interest rates, restored local elected representation at the county level, put state money into every level of local schools, spent state taxes on charitable institutions and prisons, and finally, authorized the issuance of a historical text book for public schools entitled "School History of the Negro Race in the United States."*

In the Roots of Southern Populism, Steven Hahn summarizes the five major criticisms the agrarians made against the special interest political system.

First, the agrarians understood that the increasing wealth and economic power in the market place was transferring a certain range of political privileges from economic affairs to political affairs.

That transfer of economic power translated into a political ability to exercise sovereign political power over farmers that was not in any way derived from the consent of the governed, and was not subject to reform through the mechanism of electoral politics.

The political power drew its sustenance from economic power, and was concentrated in the branches of the federal government, making local and state governments less able to ameliorate the effects of the elite's centralized power and privileges.

Second, the agrarians could see how the combination of economic power and privileges created the conditions of economic dependency for farmers. Not only was the economic growth throttle of investments in the hands of the elites, thanks to Hamilton, but the police power of the state was being used to force farmers, against their will, to remain under the tutelage of the elite, through the operation of the debt-peonage contracts and tight money policies.

Farmers could never get out of debt, were losing title to their lands, and had no path of escape and no path of upward occupational mobility.

The farmers were slaves in a new type of slavery system.

To paraphrase C. B. MacPherson, farmers had become an economic "thing," whose interests did not really matter to the elites in either party. The only interest that mattered politically was the ruling-class view of the national collectivist interest, which coincidentally, was exclusively the financial interests of the elite.

Third, the agrarians learned a tough political lesson that the machinery of the election system was totally corrupt. It was corrupt in counting votes, corrupt in casting ballots, corrupt in conducting elections, corrupt in voter registration, and corrupt in distributing the "spoils" of the elections.

It was so corrupt, that in the South, most of the formerly elected local positions were eliminated and replaced by appointments handled by the ruling Democratic Party officials in each state capital.

The corruption at the local and state level was compounded by corruption in election machinery at the federal government level. As in the case of economic debt-peonage, there was no path of escape for the farmers from the political corruption that aimed at denying them participation in the political system.

Speaking in 1858, Georgia governor Joseph Brown said, "It is already claimed by some that the banks now have the power by combinations and free use of large sums of money to control the political conventions and elections in our State, and in this way to crush those who may have the independence to stand by the rights of the people in opposition to their aggressive power."

Fourth, the populist critique of the American system contained a moral element about the worth and value of the individual. The existing value system in place at the time emphasized a person's moral worth in terms of financial wealth, and this moral worth, following Locke, translated into political decision making power.

As Bill Cecil-Fronsman pointed out, the constitution "...reminded common whites that they were members of a society whose leaders regarded wealth as a legitimate measure of a man's worth."

The agrarians, in contrast, believed that a person's worth was derived from a loving God, who loved all individuals equally.

Finally, the agrarians had learned first hand the intricate relationship between control of banking and money supply system and the legal system. They understood how credit relationships between lenders and debtors could easily be extended into debt-peonage relationships wherein debtors lost their land and ended up in prison.

The farmers could also see first hand the effect of how a change in the Homestead Laws allowed bankers and merchants to extort land titles, under the guise of the rule of law.

The Populist leaders understood how the rule of law could be subverted, as eloquently expressed by Leonidas Polk, who said,

> "To say that the unjust and ruinous exactions of capital and corporate power are made in conformity to law is no answer, for there is no tyranny so degrading as legalized tyranny, there is no injustice so oppressive as that which stands entrenched behind the forms of law."

Underlying all of these criticisms of Madison's constitutional rules of procedure is a common set of enduring social and cultural values involving individual freedom.

As noted by V. O. Key, in Southern Politics In State and Nation,

> "Philosophers and historians find the origin, if not the explanation, of this spirit in the political struggles at the end of the past century, which propelled the state (of North Carolina) into its modern era of liberalized Democratic government.
> The struggles centered around Republican and Populist forces which captured control of the state legislature in 1894 and elected a Republican governor in 1896."

According to Robert Goldwin,

> "The Anti-Federalist's great concern was that the powers of the national government threatened the annihilation of the state governments...What was a danger to all liberty was an all-powerful central government able to tax from a great distance and thus render state and local government relatively powerless."

While this value of local government over federal government started out it's political life in the Anti-Federalist, Jefferson-Republican camp, its trajectory eventually took it to a new home in the Southern-Bourbon-Democrat party.

The lesson taught here by the anti-federalists, is that the powerful central government is always a threat to liberty, and that the central government always moves in the direction of killing local and state government.

The strange trajectory and use of the value of local government from the time of the Anti-Federalists is an example of what Lawrence Goodwyn described as the opportunistic use of cultural values for short term political gain by the two

dominant parties.
Goodwyn wrote,

> "Sectional, religious, and racial loyalties and prejudices were used to organize the nation's two major parties that ignored the economic interests of millions...Thus, the many-faceted Republican coalition that came to power in 1861 became in the postwar years a much narrower business party, closely tied to the politics of sectional division...the fact was central: sectional prejudices in the 1880's and 1890's persisted as an enormous political barrier to anyone bent on creating multi-sectional party of reform."

Eugene Genovese makes the point that the value of local government as a political propaganda tool for the special interests coexisted with the Bourbon defense of slavery. "So long as the slaveholders made few demands on these upcountry (anti-federalist) regions, their claims to being champions of local freedom and autonomy against meddling outsiders appeared perfectly legitimate," to the farmers.

In the hands of the slaveholder Bourbon Democrats, the value of local government was used as a ruse for political purposes to gain and maintain elected positions.

According to Palmer, in Man Over Money, the anti-federalists and agrarians linked local government to individual sovereignty.

He wrote,

> "The essential social relationship was between individuals, not between people and organizations...they considered the social order at bottom a network of personal relationships between human beings rather than impersonal relations between people and social organizations, such as the government, labor unions, courts, and corporations."

The common whites in the South, according to Cecil-Fronsman, "...boldly asserted their independence and self-worth; they insisted that they were as good as anyone else. On the other hand, they lived in a society that made it plain that they were not."

Living in this social contradiction in the South led to many unusual arrangements and relationships between both common whites and plantation elites, and more interestingly, between common whites and free blacks.

Eventually, it was the threat posed by the political coalition of common whites and blacks, in the guise of the Populist Party, that led to the violent counter-attack of the Bourbon Democrats, using the war cry of "Negro Rule" (the

Democrats used a more vernacular term) as their rallying point.

Equality, for the agrarians, was derived from a condition of independence upon others, and freedom was achieved by acquiring sufficient land and resources to insure personal independence.

Allen Tullos commented upon this value in, Habits of Industry: White Culture and the Transformation of the Carolina Piedmont, when he noted that,

> "Farmer logic was powered by a commitment to personal independence, family self sufficiency, and neighborly interdependence...In the pursuit and maintenance of independence, the farm household itself became the yeomanry's most productive resource."

As applied to politics, the teleos, or end goal of common whites in the South, before and after the Civil War, was, according to Steven Hahn, "...a commonwealth of independent producers for whom political liberty and personal freedom were inseparable from the patterns of mutuality in their settlements."

It was Hahn's interpretation that in the Civil War the common whites "fought for a liberty and independence not beholden to slaveownership, but rooted in communities of petty producers."

The most common phrase that the Southern white soldiers used to describe this idea was "Rich man's war, poor man's fight."

Traveling through the South at the turn of the eighteenth century, Charles Jansen wrote that the common whites he met were "...extremely tenacious of the rights and liberties of republicanism. They consider themselves on an equal footing with the best people of the country and upon the principles of equality they intrude themselves into every company."

The origin of this value lay in the southern yeoman tradition of subsistence farming, that provided self-reliance and independence from the elite social classes.

Paul Escott notes, in Many Excellent People, that "North Carolina's yeomen were, in reality, a self-directed, stubborn and independent group. Theirs was a traditional way of life based upon subsistence farming. It was neither luxurious not easy, but it offered self-reliance and self-respect."

It is from the value of self-respect and independence from subsistence farming, that the farmers could gain a measure of respect and equality to others.

Escott goes on to write, that from the eyes of the plantation elite, the yeomen were not respectable, and tended to view them as unreliable and in the same class as free blacks and slaves.

This conception of common whites endured for much of the 19th century.

Edward Ayers quotes Worth Bagley, a member of the plantation elite in 1892, that the Agrarians were "...perfect upstarts who desire to bring themselves up to a level with the best, imagining (political) office will do it. I hate the whole measly lot of pudding-headed demagogues."

According to Michael Perman, in The Road to Redemption, as a part of their political subterfuge, the Democrat New South leaders, after 1900, advocated the need for farmers to be independent and self sufficient, values the farmers deeply believed.

Perman noted that, "To be prosperous, therefore, farmers must be, first, self-reliant, and, second, no longer at the mercy of external forces for their essential services and supplies...Self-reliance and independence for the individual farmer was the hallmark of the agricultural New South."

Because of their political appeal to the farmers, the Bourbon Democrats, led farmers deeper into the debt-peonage system. Freedom and independence, for the elite, meant economic growth which benefited only the elite.

In order for the elites to be free, large numbers of white and black farmers had to be denied freedom. In order to deny farmers freedom, the farmer's had to believe that the Democrat Plantation elite were actually their political allies.

The "Party of Our Fathers" combined with the Democrat New South appeal of farmer "self-reliance" proved to be an irresistible political combination for attracting the farmers to vote for Democrats.

"At issue," for the agrarians, according to Bruce Palmer, in Man Over Money, "was not private ownership of wealth and property but their concentration in a few hands. A wider distribution of private property through equalization of opportunities would correct this."

The same interpretation of the Populist value is given by Carl Degler, in The Other South, who wrote, "The Agrarians did not object to the (free market) system; they merely wanted a fair chance to prosper under it. They had been lead to believe...that America was the home of opportunity."

Writing in Progressive Farmer, the magazine that he founded, Leonidas Polk wrote "We do not wish to be rich but only want a reasonable chance that we may be able to achieve decent and respectable lives and educate our children. Surely no enemy could say anything against such a doctrine as this."

As the Agrarians soon learned, many of their political enemies had much to say against this value, and their enemies finally ended up using the value of economic opportunity to their own advantage against the farmers.

The initial reforms sought by the Agrarians aimed at correcting the abuses primarily oriented to the agricultural economic issues of farmers. Both the cooperative buying and selling programs, and Charles Macune's Sub-Treasury Plan sought reform that would correct the existing abuse of farmers in their role as neo-slaves in the debt-lien system.

At about the same time in history that these agricultural reforms were being proposed, a parallel economic vision began to be discussed in the South that involved investment in industrial mills, primarily those associated with cotton textiles.

Beginning around 1873, the North Carolina agricultural granges of Mecklinburg, Cabarrus, and surrounding counties, began discussing how they could raise the initial capital to invest in a community textile mill.

According to Phillip Wood, in Southern Capitalism, these early discussions led to a type of community venture capital mutual fund, wherein farmers pooled their savings for the investment.

"By 1878, wrote Wood, "they had accumulated ninety thousand dollars, which they planned to use to build a mill in Gaston County."

The local pooling of capital for local industrial investment soon became a matter of great fervor for the farmers. In 1873, the Greensboro paper urged the Patrons of Husbandry, also known as the Grange, to provide the organizational base upon which to encourage, create and solidify local industries.

"The aim of such an approach," wrote the editor, "was to confer the badge of civic virtue on mill building." The modern contemporary term for this pooling of capital is "crowd funding."

This local civic virtue was described by W. J. Cash, in The Mind of the South,

> "The impulse leaps from community to community, as an electric current leaps across a series of galvanic poles - sweeping the citizens into mass assembly...it actually sets yeoman farmers, to poor as individuals to provide even so much as a single share of capital, to combining in groups of a dozen for the purpose; it sets laborers to forming pools into which each man pays as little as twenty-five cents a week."

A historical description of this phenomena of local farmers raising local investment capital is contained in Glen Gilman's piece, "The Folk Build The Mills," where he wrote,

> "A relationship grew up between the communities and their mills that was, and has remained unique in an industrial region. The community built the mills, and the mills saved the communities. The mills "belong" to the communities."

The early version of local crowdfunding, as a path to economic independence, is one of the most important lessons taught by the anti-federalist agrarians.

Their local allegiance is entirely compatible with the cultural values the farmers had of local government and individual economic freedom. Those two values were conjoined with the values of upward occupational mobility and the chance to achieve a decent life in the American dream as individual freedom, equal opportunity, and the integrity and worth of the individual.

Leonidas Polk advocated, according to Stuart Noblin in his book on Polk, many small, diversified, industries for the South.

Polk said,

> "It may be that we will yet learn that diversified industries is the surest foundation of prosperity, and that to increase these we must have less politics and give a little more time to business, talk less abut Southern independence, and work harder to bring it about."

The economic independence of farmers was a threat to the elites position of centralized political and financial power.

According to Cash,

> "The burning concern thus generated in the minds of the master class met with and married with that other concern which, as we have seen, was generated in them by their own economic difficulties...brought to a full conviction...that without ever abandoning cotton growing, the arm of the land must somehow be extended."

The solution for the master class, according to Cash, was pretty simple.

For them, the economic future of the South should look just like its past.

> "Progress was being accomplished so completely within the framework of the past that the plantation remained the single great basic social and economic pattern of the South...that is exactly what the Southern factory almost invariably was: a plantation."

In order to achieve their desired goal, the master class needed to manipulate the farmer's prime value of economic opportunity to serve the needs of the elite. The pathway of attack was along the farmer's intersection of values of individualism and local allegiance to community and family.

Bruce Palmer described how the Bourbon Democrats, beginning around 1895, began

> "...an effort to reconcile individual material self interest with the welfare of the community, (which) led to the abandonment of the core of the (farmer's) former idea - that society was held together and progressed because of the action of each person's material self-interest - and moved toward a consideration of society as a group of people rather than a collection of individuals."

Within each town and community where the mill building fervor of the farmers arose, the merchants and landowners, who were already attached to the Bourbon Democrats, began assuming control over the industrial building enterprises.

The elites formed local boosterism clubs to promote their communities as a desirable location for a mill. The land owner's financial interest in this boosterism was easy to understand according to Gavin Wright. "Virtually every industrial beginning may be traced to someone's attempt to make a capital gain on property in land," by selling the land for the industrial plant.

Following Wright,

> "there was a sense in which the beneficiaries really could be seen as 'the community' ...What was most misleading about the cotton mill rhetoric was the implication that non-property owning (white) laborers and concern for their welfare played a major role" in the booster's motivations. The master class was using the appeal of "more and better jobs" for the 'community' in a way that appealed to the farmer's need for upward mobility while at the same time, undermined the farmer's traditional values of individual freedom."

The farmer's cherished value of individual freedom gave way to a new form of economic dependency that re-established the plantation hierarchy in the form of a mill paternalism.

"The essence of the mill paternalism," according to I. A. Newby, in Plain Folk In The New South, "derived not from the exploitation it facilitated but the reciprocal relationship it defined...the mill folk explained and rationalized their dependency (in a way) that enabled them to acknowledge and act on it without losing their sense of individuality and self-worth."

In other words, under the new social contract of mill paternalism, the farmer's were persuaded to give up on their values of economic freedom in exchange for the promise of "more and better jobs" free from competition with blacks, that would be delivered by the Bourbon Democrats, who assumed control over the process of industrial development.

From a values point of view, the organizational image of society was converted by the Bourbons from one that featured relationships between individuals to one that stressed the communal values of the local town, a concept very close to the hearts of the farmers.

According to Cash, "The southern textile industry stressed communal values. Its image for social relationships in mill villages was not the market but the paternalistic family."

Under the jurisdiction of the plantation elite, the mill building movement used the values of the Agrarians, individual initiative, ambition and economic independence, which led to social relationships in mill towns that featured, according to Newby, "a kind of social atomism, suspicion of strange people and new ideas, and resistance to social innovation of any sort," including the political innovations promoted by the Agrarians.

McMath points out that the plantation elite were successful at perpetuating a myth of progress associated with the mill villages that eventually turned into a myth about the virtues of industrial recruitment schemes.

The myths "...implied that commercial and industrial endeavors centered in the region's towns and cities would rejuvenate the southern economy and that the forging of a politically solid (white) South, presided over by the lords of factory, firm and plantation, would restore a Golden Age of southern politics."

The strategy of the elites in the South in subverting the mill building of the farmers is an important historical lesson taught by the anti-federalist agrarians. The elites today continue to use this same strategy, and will continue to use it as long as Madison's constitutional arrangement stays in place.

The myth of community progress perpetuated by the master class was effective in drawing the support of the mill workers away from the Populist movement and lodging it firmly in the camp of the Bourbon Democrats.

The myth was purchased at a high cost for the common white farmers, and at an appallingly high cost to Southern Blacks.

According to Cash, "...the cotton mill worker of the South would be stripped of his ancient autonomy and placed in every department of his life under the control of his employer."

The social patterns in the southern textile mill villages looked much like the ancient client/patronage social patterns that existed 2,000 years earlier.

Phillip Wood, in Southern Capitalism, cites the case in 1895, of a southern industrial recruiter making a pitch to northern textile manufacturers to move south.

In his appeal to the New England Cotton Manufacturing Association, Edmonds told the manufacturers that they could not overcome the major southern advantage, "...a large, and at that point, mostly untapped supply of poor white workers, who were docile, not given to strikes, and as a class, were anxious to find work and willing to accept much lower wages than northern operatives."

According to Cash, "...by 1910, the barons and the stockholders of the mills were exhibiting a tendency to turn a smaller proportion of the total profits back to building of more mills or the expansion of industry and business in general, and to take more for their own personal purposes."

As long as the capital investment gap created by industrial recruitment could be filled by recruiting more outside investment, the Bourbons would achieve their ultimate goal: the re-establishment of the plantation, and their unchallenged right to exercise monopoly political authority.

Once the special interests in the South had established their neo-slavery system, there was no constitutional pathway of reform of the system for the agrarians.

According to Paul Escott, the

> "Elite Democrats did more than beat back the challenge of the Agrarians, disfranchise black people, and stigmatize cooperation between Tar Heels of both races. They imposed an undemocratic electoral system, so complete and effective that all future political discourse had a restricted character."

What remains in place today in the South, according to Jack Bass and Walter DeVries, is a "...political plutocracy that lives with a progressive myth."

The historical legacy of the myth of Southern progress was turned against the farmers, and once entrenched in the political fabric, it served to continually undermine the Agrarians values of "equal rights for all and special privileges for none."

The lessons of history that the anti-federalist/Populist experience provides for creating a new constitution can be summarized into three topic headings.

First the Populist experience offers **lessons in politics** about the futility of third party movements in America that aim to compete with the Democrats and Republicans on the issue of more citizen control over the political process.

Second, the Populist efforts at economic cooperative programs and reform of the banking system teach **lessons about both the workings of the free enterprise** system in the context of a special interest political system and the cultural values of freedom that are associated with competitive free markets.

Finally, the Populist emphasis on the cultural values of equal rights and individual freedom offers **philosophical lessons about what holds societies together** in joint cooperative natural rights constitutional democracies.

POLITICAL LESSONS:

1. A new constitution must be based on an appeal to the individual's self-interest, based upon improving the individual's control over economic destiny, as the glue that holds citizens together in a shared self-government.

In the case of the Farmer's Alliance, their first goal was to improve the individual tenant farmer's welfare through cooperative group efforts that offered the hope of success. Examples of these cooperative efforts include the buyer and seller cooperatives, the jute bag boycott, and the mass educational rallies.

As noted by McMath, in Populist Vanguard, "Without the promise of direct, individual benefit through the cooperatives, most Alliance farmers would not, except for a relatively brief time, commit themselves to working for generalized political objectives."

Schwartz makes the same point, in Radical Protest and Social Structure, where he writes, "The understanding that mutual benefits can be gained only by first making mutual sacrifices is the keystone of the organization. But, this understanding is activated only when the individual firmly believes that the action will succeed."

The individual tenant farmers who made up the membership of the agrarian movement shared a financial self-interest in getting out of the debt peonage

system.
That common financial interest led them to supporting the reform of the special interest political system.

The individual farmers thought that they could benefit from a mass movement aimed at gaining control over the economic forces that controlled the debt peonage system.

As long as the tenant farmers thought that the movement was headed in a direction that improved economic control, they supported the broader political goals of the agrarian movement.

The Populist era is best interpreted as a movement of ordinary Americans trying to gain control over their lives and futures. The urge to gain control is a natural, biologically occurring reaction that happens as a result of the brain's sorting and filtering of images.

To the extent that the Agrarian leaders and later Populist leaders combined the urge for control with concrete programs that offered better financial welfare, the farmers supported the movement.

2. The new constitution must explicitly state that the core cultural values of local government, equal rights, and upward occupational mobility are goals of the constitutional system.

When the Populist appeal to the farmer's self-interest was placed in the political context of re-occurring historical values, the farmer's participated in the political movement.

This set of values tends to crop up over and over again in the American political experience, probably as a result of the unresolved philosophical dilemma created by the difference in the goals for the union between those contained in the Declaration of Independence and their subordination of those values in Madison's rules of the Constitution.

Individual farmers, among others who read the Declaration, keep thinking to themselves that the phrase "all men created equal," has certain political implications for how the government should work.

Leonidas Polk mentioned the staying power of the values in one of his speeches when he asked how long it would take for the values to be embraced and implemented in the political system. "How long will it take?...Not long, because no lie can live forever. How long?...Not long because the arm of the moral universe is long, but it bends toward justice."

The lie Polk referred to was that ordinary Americans could continue to be denied equal rights by the elites, under the rules promulgated by Madison.

The farmers understood that their core cultural values that had been embedded in the Declaration, had not been enacted in Madison's constitution.

The farmers did not understand, nor did the Populist leaders ever fully grasp, that the values in the Declaration had been co-opted and subverted by the Democrats and Republicans, and used against the farmers.

3. A new natural rights constitution that aims at greater citizen control over government must continually allow maximum citizen participation in the development of political rules and policies.

Following Jefferson, those that are bound by the rules should have the greatest say in making the rules.

Schwartz writes convincingly about the disconnect that arose between the leaders of the Populist Party and the members. When the Populist Party began acting just like the other special interest organizational structures of the Democrats and the Republicans, the farmers began acting just like the other special interest group.

The Democrats seized upon this opportunity by doing a better job of treating the farmers like a special interest group than the Agrarians, and eventually, through the clever use of the farmer's core cultural values, the Democrats eroded the farmer's political allegiance to the Populist movement.

The farmers were initially attracted to the Populist Party because the leaders had created an economic alternative to the merchant/banker crop lien system.

This alternative economic structure appealed to the farmer's urge for economic self control. According to Schwartz, "...when the banks attacked, and when the newspaper stories questioned the Exchange's economic viability, the farmer's treated the Exchange just like any other merchant: They began to shop elsewhere."

Following Schwartz, it was the desire of the Populist leadership to protect its own interests as leaders, and their newly formed belief that the leaders had superior judgment and decision making skills than the members.

This reasoning is exactly the same that underlies any elite system based upon privilege, and the tactics deployed by the leaders were exactly the same as those in the Democratic and Republican Parties.

The Populist Party leaders began to "...suppress information, suspend democratic decision making and impose a policy that benefited only a small minority."

When the leaders of the Populist Party treated the farmer's like any other special interest group, the farmer's responded like any other group: they began to vote for the political party that made the best pitch.

Citizens that participate in the development of rules and policies derive a moral obligation, based upon the brain's ability to extend trust, to voluntarily obey the rules that they give to themselves.

On the other hand, in a special interest political system whose end goal is obtaining welfare outcomes, rules are imposed by elites, and rule obedience depends on the use of the police power of the state or some other externally imposed non-voluntary, coercive mechanism, such as the one designed in the crop lien system.

4. Disorganized political interests that aim at political reform of policies can not compete effectively against the well-organized special interests of the dominant two parties, either as a non-political organization or as a special interest, such as the modern Tea Party, that attempted to organize within the institutional structure of the Republican Party.

In his analysis of southern political institutions, V. O. Key concluded that,

> *"...over the long run, the have-nots lose in disorganized politics. They have no mechanism through which to act and their wishes find expression in fitful rebellions led by transient demagogues who gain their confidence, but often have neither the technical competence not the necessary stable base of political power to effectuate a program."*

In the case of the farmer's interests, their desire for reform was antithetical to the special interests of each party that derived financial benefits from the status quo arrangement of centralized power.

The farmer's experience, in 887, could be generalized to apply to any political reform of the political system in America, in 2017.

The special interest coalitions within each dominant party agree on only one political principle, namely that the goal of the system is to perpetuate the special interest political system.

It is quite logical and understandable that the special interests in both parties would cooperate to subvert any attempt at political reform.

Schwartz noted that the farmer's interests could not "...be dependent on, or embedded in, the original system, since that system is based on the exercise of routinized power by the dominant groups. A threat to the continuing functioning of a system cannot be mounted by the system itself."

Initially, the Agrarians thought that if they could just insert "good people" who had the right set of cultural values, into the existing two-party system, that reform could be achieved and that their welfare outcomes would be improved.

According to Bruce Palmer, in Man Over Money,

> "The Southern agrarians did not realize that the government was not designed to serve the purposes of the farmers or the laborers, or of any kind of radical reformers."

In the hands of either dominant political party, the government of America is designed to hand out benefits to the special interests. The constitutional rules designed by Madison and Hamilton led to this outcome.

In 1882, a former plantation owner was quoted in Steven Hahn's book, The Roots of Southern Populism, as saying,

> "There is no principle involved in politics since the Civil War. It is only a contest between the ins and the outs for place and power and for the privilege and opportunity to rob the U. S. Treasury."

Good people, inserted into the centralized political system, who were not initially interested in robbing the treasury, were soon corrupted by the two-party political system.

The outcome was not unexpected or unanticipated during the time that Madison was writing the constitution.

John Adams predicted the outcome by noting that the constitutional rules would divide the nation into two groups, creditors and debtors. The purpose of the constitution would be to "...settle wealth and power upon a minority. It will be accomplished by a national debt, paper corporations, and offices, civil and military. These will condense king, lords and commons, a monied faction and an armed faction in one interest."

Sticking good people into this bad system will not lead to reform.

5. Any new political movement that aims at individual freedom must anticipate and prepare for the political counter-attack that aims at destroying the movement.

After the Civil War, in the South, the dominant plantation aristocracy was disorganized politically.

During the time of Federal occupation, 1865 – 1875, this disorganization led to an opportunity for the relatively new Republican Party in the South to gain strength.

Towards the end of Federal occupation, (1875), according to Otto Olsen, in Reconstruction and Redemption in the South, the Bourbon Democrats regained their political footing, and made it clear that they "...sought to destroy rather than compete with Republicanism, and that they were willing to utilize any means necessary to do so..."

A leader of the Democratic Party, in an 1874 letter to the <u>Greensboro Patriot,</u> said "We assure the Negro equality before the law, but we also assure that we will strike down the Republican Party forever."

It took the Democrats about 25 years to make good on their promise to destroy the nascent Republican Populist political movement. The Democrats undermined the Populist Party by infiltrating the farmer's organizations and subverting the political allegiance of the farmers.

In a letter of 1891, Robert Rhett wrote to North Carolina State Representative Joseph Wheeler, a Democrat and laid out the strategy for destruction of the Republican Party, "I deem it of the utmost importance, that strong and substantial Democrats throughout this District should enter the order and control it, as they readily can do, if they choose and will go to the trouble."

The Democrats resorted to violence and fraud, including a violent coup d'etat, in Wilmington to achieve their monopoly.

According to Escott, after the coup of 1898, Democratic Party leaders were quoted as saying that "we will no longer be ruled, and we will never be ruled by men of African origin."

Furnifold Simmons, Chairman of the State Democratic Party, and a long time U. S. Senator from North Carolina said in 1898, "North Carolina is a White Man's State, and White Men will rule it, and they will crush the party of Negro domination beneath a majority so overwhelming that no other party will ever dare to establish Negro rule here."
(author's note: Simmons' actual language about Negro rule was a bit more graphic).

Simmons was referring to the very brief episode of "fusion" politics when the Populist Party formed an alliance with the Republicans, in 1894, to win the

Governor's office.

Governor Russell appointed several blacks to political office, and in several local races, like Wilmington, black people were elected to the city council.

This same language of violence and hatred that was used by the Democrats, in 1898 against Republicans, is used today by socialist Democrats today vilify Tea Party conservatives, and Republicans, and for exactly the same purposes.

Furnifold Simmons solicited campaign contributions from "...the bankers, railroad executives, lawyers and manufacturing interests, and promised that the Democrats would not raise corporation taxes if the Democrats regained power."

The Democrats made good on their promise not to raise corporate taxes, preferring always to shift the burden to common citizens through the use of sales and property taxes.

6. The new political movement of individual freedom should never underestimate what their political adversaries will do to maintain political power.

Escott notes that in North Carolina the

> *"Democratic Party resorted to fraud and force to safeguard its power and then designed a final, undemocratic political and social solution. This solution - segregation and disfranchisement - eviscerated the coalition of poorer whites and blacks and insured that established interests would not be threatened in the future."*

Among the many non-violent tactics deployed by the Democrats was the simple step of taking away elected offices and replacing them with appointments made from the central Democrat party headquarters in Raleigh.

As noted by Escott, the Democrats also took away black citizen's right to vote, limited the right of common whites to vote, and changed the election laws on how votes would be counted, primarily by election officials appointed by the central Democratic headquarters in Raleigh.

The use of violence included assassinations of Republican officials, threats of assassinations of Populist leaders, including the attempted assassination of Governor Russell, and routine lynchings of black leaders.

The violence of the Democrats in North Carolina also included forced sterilization of black people who were considered too insane to have children. The phrase used by the Democrats for insane black people was "uppity" blacks who had voted with the white Republicans.

The forced sterilization of black people in North Carolina, by the Democrats, finally ended in the mid-1970s. By that time, 50,000 black people, both males and females, had been sterilized.

As a political strategy, the forced sterilization of uppity blacks was a huge success for the Democrats. With all the genetics of uppity Blacks purged from society, Blacks in North Carolina now vote almost 100% for the Democrats.

Much of the violence of the Plantation elite took place under the auspices of the Klan, whose leadership mirrored the leadership of the Democratic Party. During the day, the prominent Democrats held elected offices and wielded official power.

At night, they would don their sheets and hoods and terrorize the black population. In an enduring historical irony, the Democrats were successful in tagging the Klan violence as perpetrated by the racist Republicans.

The lesson that this routine use of violence taught the common whites was, according to Escott,

> *"...that extralegal violence was not only effective but also a valid means of nullifying government policy and law." The violence destroyed the essence of the "rule of law" in a democracy.*

The rule of law depends upon widely held moral notions and values that every one is subject to the law and will voluntarily obey the law.

Once destroyed, the "rule of law" cannot be re-created.

As noted, after the election of 1898, by John Bassett, a keen observer and critic of North Carolina's Bourbon Democrats, the tactics used by the Democrats taught the farmers an important political lesson.

The election, said Bassett, is "one more step in the educating of our people that it is right to lie, to steal, and to defy all honesty in order to keep a certain party in power."

7. A new political movement that aims at promoting individual freedom and more citizen control over the affairs of government must first establish a territorial stronghold in local governments.

The leaders of the agrarian movement recognized that concentrated economic power in America combined with centralized political power in Washington, D. C. limited the economic opportunities of farmers. Before them, the anti-federalists made this same argument.

Part of the early appeal of the Populist Party was related to the farmer's cultural value orientation to local autonomy and their preference for local government related to their fear of the national central government.

This value orientation of the farmers is related to the insight provided by Lawrence Goodwyn, in Democratic Promise: The Populist Movement In America. It was through personal participation in shared hopes for reform at the local community level that provided the farmers with their early sense of optimism and faith that reform could be achieved.

When the Democrats counter-attacked the Agrarians, it was this shared sense of hope and joint participation in local affairs that they aimed to destroy.

Escott explains that the point of this attack was easy to understand.

> *"It is easy to see why the Democratic offensive was aimed so directly at local government. Control of county affairs had been the foundation of North Carolina's aristocratic social order...In February of 1877, the legislature abolished elected county government and put local power back into the hands of appointed officials."*

By centralizing political power in the southern state capitals, the Democrats eliminated the source of strength for farmer's to organize a political opposition party at the local level. Without a local level political organization, the farmers could not eradicate the national central government's power over their lives.

According to V. O Key,

> *"For a two-party system to operate effectively each party must, almost of necessity, have a territorial stronghold in which it can win legislative elections and control local government. The powers exercised by the central government of Virginia over local officials make it difficult to found an opposition faction or control of local government."*

The trends in centralization of power at the state level complemented the centralization of political power in the nation's capital.

The Democratic Party acted as the institutional mechanism to coordinate the centralization of power between the states and the centralized national government.

In the early years, the major issue used by the Democrats as a tactic for subordinating local government to the central government revolved around eliminating the threat of Negro Rule associated with the Republican Party.

According to Key,

> "...the predominate consideration in the architecture of southern political institutions has been to assure locally a subordination of the Negro population and externally, to block threatened interferences from the outside with these local arrangements."

Once the citizens at the local level became accustomed to looking through the Democratic Party to the state capital, and then to the nation's capital for special interest welfare improvements, their sense of dependency on the special interest system grew over time.

As noted above, the Democrats played upon the farmer's traditional values of local government to achieve the centralization of power at both the state and national level.

According to Perman, the Democrats appealed to the "...right of particular political and social entities to pursue their own course without restraint or hindrance" from outside forces.

In the hands of the Democrats, this appeal translated into non-interference with state Democrats, by the national government, on the Democrat's efforts to eliminate both the Populist and the Republican Party.

It is through personal participation in developing rules and laws at the local level, however, which contribute to an individual's sense of control. Local government acts as a forum for citizens to build political efficacy in managing their civic affairs.

As a result of this sense of control, citizens at the local government level develop the strength and courage to withstand the encroachments of power brought about by the forces of centralization inherent in Madison's constitution.

A political movement that seeks to redirect power away from the central government should first seek an elected base at the local level, and then anticipate a violent counter-attack by the established political powers.

Economic Lessons of History

1. Hard work, by itself, does not insure financial success or lead to upward occupational mobility in the existing constitutional arrangement.

Both black and white farmers were used to working hard, and long hours, before the Populist Party appeared.

In the minds of many farmers who were attracted to the agrarian movement, hard work was associated with the value of independence and the moral value of a person.

In the Savage Ideal, Bruce Clayton notes that in the South, "work was a moral absolute, an outer sign of inner worth..."

It should be noted that this value of work was not shared by the Plantation aristocracy, who generally abhorred physical work as a sign of social weakness.

The farmers learned a tough lesson about work after the Civil War, as the debt-peonage system tightened its grip.

The lesson was captured by Goodwyn, in his article, "The Cooperative Movement."

> "At settlin' up time, the farmer and the merchant would meet at the cotton gin, where the fruits of year's toil would be ginned, bagged, tied, weighed, and sold. At that moment, the farmer would learn what his cotton had brought. The merchant, who had possessed title to the crop, even before the farmer had planted it, then consulted his ledger for a final time. The accumulated debt for the year, he informed the farmer, exceeded the income from the crop."

The farmer, in the vernacular of the time, had "failed to payout." There was no escape, no way out of debt. The debt-lien laws held the farmer on the land for the next year, in the new slavery system, and would keep him there, year after year.

As the crop-lien system collapsed, under the tight money policies that devastated the commodity agriculture system, the hard-working farmers were offered a new form of slavery, as low wage mill workers.

This new system was even more vicious than the crop-lien system in that it captured the whole family. Rather than paying each worker a wage, the mill owners would pay a family wage, but not in cash.

The family wage was paid in script, only redeemable at the mill store, owned by the mill owner.

According to Phillip Wood, the family would have its wages withheld for a period of four weeks, during which time "they would have accumulated four weeks' debt for supplies at the company store at increased 'advance' prices."

Every member of the family, beginning at age 6, worked in the mill, usually for 16 hours per day, and like the debt-peonage system of the farm, the family never got out of debt and had no economic path of escape.

In Habits of Industry, Tullos describes the "...historical process in which the industrial fathers held a strong upper hand over desperate families who came to the mills already accustomed to long days and years of punishing physical labor for little reward."

According to Tullos, the farmers, both on the farm and later in the mills, learned, that "by itself, hard work could establish little."

The value of hard work among the farmers, though, was soon picked up as a public relations ploy of the New South Democrats, and used against the farmers, like so many of their other core values.

In an 1886 speech to northern industrialists, Henry Grady began by saying that in the South "We have fallen in love with work."

As described by Lawrence Shore, what Grady was trying to do was explain to the northerners how the New South, with its cheap white labor, could benefit the northern industry.

The New South boosters added one new element to the hard work value. Not only did the mill workers work hard, they were also faithful and docile, nearly an unbeatable combination for northern elites.

Beginning around 1895, the northern industry began moving south. According to Wood, "The capital came South because the profit margin in the South was much greater than in the North. While the Carolina mills showed profits of 10 to 30%, profits in the 1890's and 1900's averaged 5.83% in the U. S. and 7.7% in New England."

As noted above, the profits were never reinvested into the Southern economy, creating an investment capital gap that, over time, left both Southern workers and the Southern economy, poor, despite the widely-shared cultural value of hard work.

It was this blatant exploitation of labor, and the misuse of the cultural values of hard work, that prompted Tom Watson, in 1891, to ask in his newspaper, "What is Labor's fair share?" he answered by saying that labor should "get all it makes after due allowance for material and the use of capital."

Watson and other Populist leaders believed that the government should act on behalf of labor in securing this fair share.

The economic lesson from the Populist experience is that neither hard work, by itself, nor the government, acting in a special-interest driven system, will secure a fair share or reward based upon merit.

2. Monopoly power in the banking credit system, combined with monopoly power in the capital investment process, lead to an economic system with no path of economic advancement for the farmers.

Hamilton was right in his analysis of the importance of investment capital as the engine of economic growth in an industrial economy. His insistence on securing the loyalty of investors and bankers made a lot of sense *for the northern economy.*

The southern economy, however, was not industrial, and most of its working capital was held in a peculiar institutional bank, called slavery.

After the Civil War, the South did not have liquid financial capital in the same way that the North did, yet the South was forced to compete on the terms and conditions set by the northern bankers.

Given the hard money policy of the national Republicans, which limited the circulation of currency, and given the massive spending programs implemented by the newly installed Republicans in Southern states, most southern states ran up huge debts, which required hard currency to repay.

Beginning in the mid-1870's, the southern states starting defaulting on this debt.

According to Perman, in The Road to Redemption,

> *"...the public debts that were being renounced had been incurred for the very reason that the South did not have any private capital of its own to draw on...it would be forced into utter reliance on outside resources...external capital tended to consolidate and control the southern economy...the South had in effect, surrendered control over its future economic development."*

The terms and conditions of this surrender were entirely satisfactory to the Plantation elite.

In exchange for northern industrial capital, the plantation aristocracy would deliver a docile hard working white workforce.

According to Wood, for southern Bourbon Democrats, "the ability to reduce wages and implement the stretch-out (extending the work day to 16 hours), was the key to high rates of surplus value and, ultimately, to the ability to attract large amounts of new capital."

As long as both parties to the contract kept their side of the deal, the North agreed not to interfere with the Southern political system of apartheid.

Initially, what the farmers wanted was equal access to capital. What they found, according to Stephen Hahn, was a territorial financial monopoly, "which prevented competition in the extension of credit, and a monopoly over the sources of necessary credit in a system increasingly dominated by staple agriculture."

This last element of monopoly had a handy title of "no cotton, no credit."

The system of monopoly capital in the South, both on the farm, and later in the mills, eliminated one part of the American dream for the farmers. They were trapped, with no path of escape.

According to Walter Hines Page, a critic of the Bourbon Democrats, who moved safely away to New York, to criticize from a distance, the plantation aristocracy had placed shackles on the southern (white) society.

> *"There is absolutely no chance for the ambitious men of ability, proportionate to their ability. North Carolina was falling behind because it refused to give every man a chance in making intellectual and social progress."*

One of the policies implemented by the Republican-Populist Governor Daniel Russell was an examination of how the monopoly of northern capital, used in the industrial recruitment schemes of the Bourbon Democrats, eroded the "public purpose" of the state.

After the Democratic victory of 1898, Russell spent the rest of his life embroiled in a legal controversy over how private financial interests in North Carolina were taking advantage of public resources to serve special private interests.

The Populist response to the financial monopoly was to create competitive alternatives in the form of the Agrarian Cooperative Exchanges and the Sub-Treasury system.

These programs tended to open up pathways of occupational mobility for farmers, and thus, constituted a threat to the plantation aristocracy's position of monopoly power.

The monopoly power was used to restrain geographical and occupational mobility of the farmers. The farmers could not obtain credit to finance independent business activities, and could not get out of debt under the conditions created by the monopoly.

In response to the competitive threat posed by the Populist alternatives, the Democrats counter-attacked. In 1893, they changed the state law to make it illegal for the Farmer's Alliance to engage in the business of the cooperative exchanges, and then, in 1898, they permanently eliminated the threat posed by the Populist Party by implementing apartheid.

3. The combination of monopoly power over credit and monopoly power in politics allowed the Democrats to create an economic system by the few, for the few.

In order for the economic system of the Democrats to function, it was absolutely necessary for them to restrict occupational mobility and to keep the white labor force near poverty levels.

As noted by Cash,

> "Whatever the intent of the original founders of progress, the plain truth is that everything here rested finally upon one fact alone: cheap labor...the wages were on average just about adequate to the support of a single individual - such wages as required that every member of a family moving from the land into Factory-town, who was not incapacitated by disease or age or infancy, should go into the mills in order that he too might eat."

Beginning in the mid 1890's, the Democrats began using the political rhetoric that " a low wage job is better than no job at all," to remind white workers that the Democratic Party was their friend in recruiting low wage jobs.

The Democrats began using the agencies of state government in increasingly elaborate schemes to recruit low wage industry to the South.

As described by Cash,

> "What with free sites and waiving of taxes, about all the South was getting out of the removal of the New England mills was the stingy sums paid in wages (to the southern mill workers)...The increased employment was a boon of sorts, perhaps. But a boon purchased at the appalling prices of virtually giving away the inherent resources of the section, physical and human."

The recruitment of low wage, semi-skilled jobs, using tax incentives, according to Cash "gave away the wealth of the South on a scale hitherto unprecedented in a region which has always too eagerly given away its wealth. And, it exacts no adequate advantage...the people who mainly gain from it are the merchants and bankers."

These "merchants and bankers" were the same set of actors who implemented the crop-lien system, and then successfully shifted strategy when the cotton economy died, in order to implement the industrial recruitment strategy.

In their capacity as elected leaders, the merchants and bankers used the agencies of state government both to restrict the movement of labor and to give away the state's resources to northern and foreign manufacturers as incentives for them to build manufacturing plants in the south.
According to Wood,

"The State (of North Carolina) is thus a result of the history of class struggle while at the same time a participant in it. It (the state government) must secure the conditions necessary for capital accumulation in a context of class conflict and by means that are themselves conditioned by class conflict."

One of the ways the Democrats gave away the state's resources, according to Ayers, in the Promise of the New South, was by continually promising business interests that they would not raise corporate income taxes.

The Democratic promise included "low taxes on railroads and farmlands, with few restrictions on business and few demand on government." One of the 'few restrictions" on business included no restrictions on how young a person could be to work in the mill, nor how long the children could work.

Furthermore, by keeping taxes low, and encouraging child labor at age six, the Democrats did not spend money on the public education system.

The low wage, semi-skilled work force did not require education in order to be productive in this economic system.

Gavin Wright observed that as long as the Democratic Party could segregate the white workers from the black workers in the system of state-sanctioned apartheid, the working of the labor market itself would function to keep wages low.

Wright cites the

> *"evidence that indicates that farm and industrial unskilled labor markets were closely linked. The equilibrating pressures of a competitive labor market were vividly illustrated by the convergence of wages for white males in the cotton textile plants and black males in tobacco manufacturing."*

What was new about this economic system was the dynamic between racially segregated labor markets, that kept wages low, and that offered no opportunities for advancement for either blacks or whites.

The system was held together by the constant threat by the Democratic leaders that Negroes would be used to replace white workers in the textile mills, an effective economic use of racism derived from a position of Democratic Party political monopoly.

The lesson that the farmers and Agrarians learned from this system is that if they ever voted for Republicans or Agrarians again, they would lose their jobs, thus giving credence to the Democratic ploy that a "low wage job was better than no job at all."

As an alternative economic development strategy, Leonidas Polk had expressed his interest in the creation of many small, diversified industries in the South. His comments came during the time that farmers in small towns were raising capital to invest in community mills.

The initiative for the policy of locally-owned mill building originated many years earlier in North Carolina, and has been expressed throughout the state's history as the "growth from within" strategy.

Dwight Billings notes that as early as 1828, the North Carolina House of Commons discussed how the state's economy could generate more opportunities for its citizens, while decreasing the economic dependency on outside capital. In one passage from the minutes of that delegation, a passage read,

> *"In setting about to ameliorate our condition the first step is to adopt some system that will enable us to buy less and sell more - that will enable us to supply within ourselves, our own wants and necessities...Instead of sending off at great expense of our transportation, our raw material, convert it into fabrics at home, and in that state, bring it to market...the manufacturing system will become our greatest means of wealth and prosperity: it will change the course of trade, and, in a great measure, make us independent of Europe and the North."*

Echoes of this early policy emphasis on growth from within, and the cultural value of economic independence for citizens are heard at various moments in history.

In 1946, Governor Gregg Cherry called for the establishment of "...more small industries, community industries, which will use local capital, local labor, and local raw materials, the goal of which is to have a great number of new businesses, born of our own money and brains and pretty closely related to our agricultural life in this state."

As recently as 1986, a legislative task force on economic development stated that North Carolina must be more aggressive in pursuing a growth from within strategy to complement industrial recruitment.

Josh Busby, in Evolution of North Carolina's Economic Development, noted that critics of the state's economic system by the few for the few observed that the growth from within strategy would "be naive if local elites are allowed to control the pace of economic and social change."

That is exactly the lesson taught by the Populist experience in their attempt to change the monopoly economic and political power of the Bourbon Democrats.

Escott quotes a farmer, J. A. Wilson, from Mecklinburg County, N. C., in 1894, "Owing to legislation in favor of monopolies, our lands are gradually slipping away from the hands of the wealth-producing classes and going into the hands of the few."

The ownership of land was concentrated in the hands of the few, the capital was in the hands of the few, and government decisions were in the hands of the few, all of which resulted in no economic opportunities for the many.

The Agrarians discovered that when all the power of the state, the banks, and investment capital, are deployed in an integrated strategy aimed at maintaining the system of unequal rights and special privileges, that political reform is futile.

4. In the absence of freely competitive labor markets and price competition, the benefits of the free enterprise system do not extend to non-elites.

Steven Hahn wrote that the Agrarians advocated public regulation of production and exchange relationships, and promoted government ownership of the means of transportation and communication.

Critics of the Agrarians, including the Bourbon Democrats, used the advocacy of these policies to argue that the Agrarians were really socialists, who were intent on overthrowing the government of America.

The Democrats were successful in tying the threat of socialism with the even greater threat of "Negro Rule" to wean the farmers and mill workers away from the Republican and the Populist Party.

The Populist advocacy of government ownership of the certain segments of production and distribution is quite logical, given the legal barriers to economic advancement created by the Democrats.

Beginning in 1876, the Democrats throughout the South began passing a series of laws, known as "anti-enticement laws" that made it illegal to entice a farmer from the land of his Landlord, or to "aid or abet" the farmer in transportation from the land.

In conjunction with the Landlord-Tenant Acts, which made it a felony to remove crops from the land without the Landlord's approval, the system of laws in the South were effective at eliminating opportunities for economic advancement.

As noted by Wood, the combination of laws, "allowed the planters to create a labor force whose freedom was severely curtailed by the indebtedness arising from the operation of the lien system and reinforced by the actions of the State."

One of the lessons learned by the Agrarians was that looking to the "State" for help in solving their problems was not an effective strategy. The "state," and especially the police power of the state, in the hands of the progeny of the plantation did not function as an agency that created equal rights for all and special privileges for none.

There was nothing in the constitutions of the states or in Madison's constitution that directed the state to function in this manner.

The purpose of the state in Madison's scheme evolved as a system to create citizen dependency on the special interest welfare system, not promote independence through upward occupational mobility.

The Agrarians learned that the police power of the state was an effective agent of the ruling elite in keeping labor mobility and economic freedom restricted.

According to Wood, when the mill workers finally rebelled, beginning in 1929, the progeny of the plantation rolled out the police to enforce the economic conditions of the mills.

In Gastonia, N.C., the local police attacked a tent colony for evicted workers, and a striking mother of five children was shot and killed by the police. O. Max Gardner, Governor at the time, and the owner of a textile mill in Cleveland County, sent in 5 companies of state militia, including cavalry and a howitzer battery to break the strike.

In Marion, striking workers were attempting to flee an onslaught by local police when six workers were shot and 25 were seriously wounded. All of the dead workers had been shot in the back.

In Elizabethtown, N. C., striking mill workers were confronted by 800 state police and deputy sheriffs, who were paid directly by the mills and equipped with National Guard equipment. The police were under the command of the mill's superintendent.

The same bloody, violent story could be told over and over again throughout the South, as mill workers learned the lesson that the benefits of free enterprise and competition do not work so well if they are not backed by a set of cultural values and certain constitutional rights.

The lesson they learned is that in order for the benefits of free competition to work, workers must be free economically to seek their own greatest advantage, and that the police power of the state must not be used against them to keep them in a poverty-stricken state of dependence.

As it turned out, the Agrarians learned that when the constitution is silent on these matters, the benefits associated with the invisible hand of free markets do not automatically extend to non-elites.

PHILOSOPHICAL LESSONS

1. There is a deep, unabiding philosophical hostility in America's natural aristocracy towards the "fitness" of certain individuals to participate in government decisions.

In his analysis of how the Bourbon Democrats destroyed the Populist Party, V. O. Key noted that the system of apartheid imposed on the South was not simply about "white supremacy."

He said, "the issue of Negro suffrage is a question not of white supremacy but the supremacy of which whites."

The philosophy that undergirded the Democratic assault combined their view that Blacks were an inferior race with the view that common whites were unfit to govern.

The "fusion" of economic and political interests between blacks and whites, according to the Democrats, had to be destroyed in order to preserve the Democrat's view of "sound government."

The philosophical hostility towards certain individuals originated in the unresolved differences between the values about individual freedom and happiness contained in the Declaration of Independence and the absence of those values in Madison's constitutional rules.

At their essence, the differences have to do with the interpretation of "natural" rights versus "political" rights.

This difference in interpretation was eloquently expressed by the North Carolina Bourbon Democratic jurist, Thomas Ruffin, in 1866. "The natural rights," said Ruffin, "inherent in freedom entitled people to security in person and property under the law; but political rights were 'conventional' not 'natural' because they involved powers over the Constitution and laws and were granted according to the sense of the community of the fitness of particular classes."

The Democrats believed that if certain "unfit" people participated in government, the result would be "anarchy."

As a former North Carolina plantation owner and Governor-elect Jonathan Worth expressed it in 1868,

> *"The tendency is to ignore virtue and property and intelligence and to put the powers of government in the hands of mere numbers...The majority in all times and in all countries are improvident and without property. Agrarianism and anarchy must be the result of this ultra democracy."*

Agrarian opponents of the Democrats understood exactly where this anti-democratic philosophy would lead. According to a 1868 editorial in the Randolph Sun, "Democrats say the ignorant people are not fit to choose their own officers. Is that right? No, it involves a principle of tyranny and oppression."

The Democrats feared the "anarchy" and "agrarianism" of majority rule, and began as early as 1875, to implement the elements of tyranny and oppression. Their work was finally completed in their masterpiece of apartheid, that lasts even to current times.

What the Agrarians learned from this experience is that cultural values and morality matter a great deal in directing the affairs of society. Under one set of cultural values, individual natural rights extended to political and constitutional rights.

As captured by Jefferson, these values were

> *"...to maintain the will for the majority of the convention and of the people themselves. We believed, with them, that man was a rational animal, endowed by nature with rights and an innate sense of justice:*

> *and that he could be restrained from wrong and protected in right, by moderate powers, confided to persons of his own choice and held to their duties by dependence on his own will."*

The set of cultural values associated with the notion that certain people are unfit to govern leads not only to tyranny, but to a centralization of power, a trend easily seen by de Tocqueville as early as 1837.

He concluded that "statism" was the promise of American life leading to a "concentration of power and the subjection of individuals..."

Albert Bushnell Hart, wrote in, 1910 The Southern South, that "southerners lived under a rigid hierarchy of elite domination: in no other region did a small aristocracy exercise such prestige and influence...in the South, the well-to-do, the cultured, the educated and the well connected absolutely controlled society."

The lesson learned by the Agrarians was that their philosophical enemies did not share any of Jefferson's notions or values. Once the elites obtained monopoly control of the reins of government, the Democrats provided not just a system of elite decision-making, but a cultural collectivism that reinforced the notion that certain people were unfit to govern, whether they were black or white.

As Key observed, it was not just a question of white supremacy, but which whites would reign supreme.

And, as time went on, the Democrats showed how adept they were at manipulating collectivist values and welfare programs to maintain their political monopoly in Madison's special interest-driven system.

The collectivism of the elites allowed the Democrats to break the economic and social relationships between southern blacks and whites.

In 1918, according to Reverend Will Alexander, of Nashville, Tennessee, quoted by William Link, "Among the lower rungs of the social order, the races freely mixed."

Writing in 1922, in <u>The Journal of Social Forces,</u> Ashby Jones connected the paternalism of the plantation elites to the cultural collectivism that viewed all blacks as a social class.

> *"Although upper-class whites had inherited a benevolent feeling toward the individual Negro, they expressed a social and political fear of the race en masse.*

This dehumanization of blacks among the better classses of southern whites was responsible for the unspeakable record of barbaritees committed against this weaker race."

The Agrarians learned that the cultural values of collectivism, that views individuals solely as a part of a undifferentiated group, both contributed to centralized political and economic power, and was an effective weapon for controlling both blacks and whites, who were seen as collectivist groups "not fit" to participate in political decisions.

The threat of "Negro Rule" was effective for the Democrats because it conjured up a mental image for white workers that their interests, as a collectivist group, were threatened by blacks, as seen as a collectivist group.

Once the Democrats were successful in having both blacks and whites view each other as collectivist groups, their special interest political system became much more effective at maintaining political power.

The philosophy of collectivism continues to work well for modern Democrats in controlling the loyalties of blacks and other "disadvantaged groups" by continually invoking class warfare and continually increasing welfare dependency of the groups upon a government controlled by the elites.

2. In order to be politically successful, the Populist Party's efforts at empowering common citizens depended upon a matrix of shared cultural values involving the "rule of law," trust, truth, morality and faith in God. The Agrarians naively believed that these truths were self-evident and that everyone, even their philosophical enemies, shared these values.

Under one set of cultural values, the primacy of individual freedom seemed self-evident to the Agrarians. If those cultural values had been supported by a certain set of constitutional rules, then the Agrarians may have experienced more success in competing with the Democrats and Republicans.
However, one of the lessons learned by the Agrarians, and valuable for any other third party reform movement, is that the set of rules devised by Madison and Hamilton are not undergirded by these values.

The constitutional deck in America is stacked against political reform, and the cultural values of truth, trust and morality held by the Agrarians are not widely-shared.

The most elemental value held by the Agrarians was that the moral teachings in the Judeo-Christian heritage was that individual morality was built into human reason.

From the Christian teachings, the Agrarians derived the notion that trust in others would be extended in the absence of evidence that it would be reciprocated. The Agrarians were both trusting of others and had faith that the righteousness of their cause would be vindicated.

In his sermons warning against the Democrat's White Man's Rule, John Kilgo, the President of Trinity College, from 1894 - 1910, preached that "God sets no limits upon the rights of men to know the truth, but rather stirs them with the energies of His spirit to search it out. God, of all beings, has little patience with, or tolerance of, a timid search for the truth."

The Agrarians shared this idea of truth, and believed that if common citizens could be shown the truth, that they would act upon the truth in building a moral and just society.

As described by Richard Tuck, in Natural Rights Theories, the Agrarians thought that man's relationship to each other and to the world was conceptually the same as God's relationship. Individuals, by using all of their intellectual and spiritual resources, could create God's Kingdom on earth.

The relationship between God and man, in the Populist theology, was a reciprocal one between equals, which generated rights and obligations on both sides. The Populist thought that this reciprocity and obligation in equal rights extended, naturally, to constitutional and political relationships.

As noted in Bruce Palmer's book, Man Over Money, the Agrarians would often invoke the teaching of Jesus in their political teachings. "Christ did not come, said one Populist leader in 1894, "as our theological quacks are so fond of saying, to prepare men for another world, but to teach them how to rightly live in this one."

Dr. Cyrus Thompson said that Christianity was the "very genius of human freedom," and criticized the southern church for failing to support the Agrarians.

Marion Butler, the Populist leader from North Carolina, said "A Christianity that cannot go down to the root causes from which poverty and oppression come is a stench in the nostrils of Jesus Christ."

Speaking on behalf of the Democrat status quo, Reverend Edwin Yates, of the Methodist Raleigh District, said that the southern church had to stand against the anarchy and nihilism represented by the Populist movement. The church "but can align itself with the powers that be, for they are ordained of God...The business of the church is to save souls, not to rectify government or make civil laws."

The powers that be saw the farmers, the blacks, females and all non-elites, as appendages to social groups, not as individuals.

Speaking to blacks in 1878, the Democratic leaders of Wilmington wrote in the Wilmington Post, "If the colored people will trust us and vote with us, we will act for their interests just as we do for the interests of the women and minors who do not vote at all."

Just trust us, and we will take care of you was the political prescription of the Democrats, and once they figured out the power of the formula, the values of truth, trust, and morality in politics became irrelevant.

Many of the southern representatives to the Constitutional Convention accurately foresaw the dangers of Madison's rules.

As Merrill Jensen pointed out in The Making of the American Constitution, George Mason insisted that Madison's restrictive process of amending the constitution was a danger to individual liberty.

The rules, said Mason, gave "ultimate control, and no amendment could ever be obtained by the people, if the government became oppressive, as he said it would."

What the Populist theology was aimed at was not being taken care of by elites, but having a moral relationship with others, based upon their conception of their relationship with God. As Michael Tuck's observation pointed out, the Populist theology, applied to the political system combined the elements of federalist republicanism with the Whig philosophy about local government.

In this combination,

> "Government was a trust, set up to serve the interests of the governed, best achieved by making the interests of the governed and the governors identical. The public interest is the honoring of the trust that is government, that the interest of each is the interest of all. Perfectly rational beings would devote themselves to the public good so understood."

The Populist sought public consent and popular control, and believed that God's design of human hearts and human brains would allow for voluntary cooperative behavior. As they learned, their philosophical enemies labored under no such lofty illusions. Government, and politics, was simply about obtaining and maintaining power.

In an irony of history, the elite collectivism of the Democratic Party resurrected the concept of "virtual representation" that the British King had used to suggest that the colonist's interests were represented in Parliament, even without a real life representative.

In virtual representation, citizens do not need to vote or participate, because the elites, who know what is good, will take care of the citizens.

Madison's flaw would have it no other way.

In his article, "The Ninth Amendment and Contemporary Jurisprudence," Edward Erler noted that "constitutional government means that the people retain the mass of sovereign power and delegate only certain portions of that sovereignty in the form of enumerated powers to government."

The decisions of the majority in this constitutional arrangement are legitimate to the extent that they are directed to the larger philosophical goals of individual freedom, undergirded by allegiance to the rule of law.

In order for that type of constitutional government to work, there must be widely-shared cultural values about individual freedom. The conflicts and tensions over the unique set of cultural values that support individual freedom are the same as they have been since antiquity.

As noted by Jefferson, all men are "naturally divided into two parties. Those who fear and distrust the people are opposed by men who identify themselves with the people, have confidence in them, and consider them as honest and safe...the Aristocrats and Democrats are the same parties still, and pursue the same object."

Madison's Federalist flaw was that he feared the people, in their capacity as individual citizens, and as a result, the centralized tyranny has become an embedded reality in America.

It was not, however, a special interest tyranny of elites, it was a socialist tyranny.

The lessons of history taught by the agrarian experience is that the only way out of the tyranny is to start over, aiming at a new government that promotes equal rights for all and special privileges for none.

Chapter 2.
The Agrarian's Arguments Against Unfair Constitutional Rules of Procedure

The agrarian's beliefs about individual morality and fairness led them to repeat, over and over again, a complaint about the American political system. Their complaint is based upon the fundamental paradox about America's political principles.

Their repetition of their complaint is based upon a mistake they made in their starting assumption that the American political system would generate outcomes that were fair to non-elites.

The agrarians never came to grips with the reality of how unfair Madison's constitutional rules were because they so deeply believed in their initial assumptions about the moral principles in the founding of the republic.

This type of repeated disbelief is similar to the repetition today by constitutional conservatives that the media is so hypocritical in its failure to investigate the abuses of the central government perpetrated by the socialist elites.

Americans in 1885, just as today, find it nearly impossible to believe that the elites and the media would not fulfill their moral obligations. The farmers never fully grasped the fact that the values in the Declaration had been co-opted and subverted by the Democrats and Republicans, and were being used against the farmers.

The irony of this part of American history is that in order to pursue the public purpose of the farmer's freedom from the debt-peonage system, the new Populist Party had to look and act like one of the two special interest political parties.

Because Madison's conception of society was borrowed from the British social class category of economics, Madison's constitutional rules demand that special interest elites continuously negotiate the "public" purpose.

Just like in the British parliamentary system, where the House of Lords negotiates the public interest, on behalf of the King, except that in America, there is no parliamentary system.

In America, political alternatives are ranked and ordered from the perspective of which alternative provides the greatest welfare benefit to the political party that happens to control the reins of government, at that moment.

As soon as the Populists tried to look and act like a special interest political party, it too became corrupted by the constitutional system created by Madison.

The Populist Party attempted to appeal to the farmers, as if they were just like any other special interest group.

Madison's rules substituted a principle of shared plunder and greed to exploit the system for the rules of the Articles of Confederation, which were based upon a shared cultural sense of fairness.

From Madison's point of view, when the proprietors of labor left the state of nature to form the social contract, they agreed that the purpose of the contract was to establish rules governing economic exchange relationships, and that the new government must have power to enforce the orderly mechanisms of market exchange.

Madison was primarily concerned with rules that would separate powers in a national government to the end that the government would be more effective than the rules established by the Articles of Confederation.

Separation of powers, by itself, does not establish allegiance to follow the rule of law.

The Rule of Law means that Americans can trust other Americans not to take advantage of them in financial and economic transactions. More importantly, the Rule of Law states that Americans can trust other citizens not do something that undermines the sovereign national commonwealth provided by the original endowment of individual liberty.

In The Natural Rights Republic, Michael Zuckert calls Madison's constitutional rules "institutional instrumentalism." This description means that Madison deals with the institutional rules that are instrumental in effecting the distribution of power in the republic.

For Madison, the purpose of government is not to provide a mechanism of rights claims and reciprocation of trust.

Rather, Madison's rules were the instruments to balance and check factional political power in order to insure that social elites, the natural leaders, who made important decisions on behalf of all society, were insulated from the tyranny that could be imposed by the people, through democratic procedures.

For the farmers, rights were claims, and social justice was achieved through fair rules of adjudicating conflict and promoting cooperation.

After the non-elites left the state of nature, and civil society had been created, the constitution, the farmers thought, would establish a mechanism to continually evaluate the justice of the civil society.

The constitution would contain rules to describe how this on-going institutional mechanism for the evaluation of the justice of the system of rights would occur, much like the existing constitution provides the framework for judicial rules of procedure.

This mistaken belief by the farmers about fair rules of exchange would have been true in the natural rights republic. It was not true in Madison's flawed arrangement, but the farmers kept trying to apply their earlier belief to their conditions, in 1887.

As explained by C. B. MacPherson, in The Political Theory of Possessive Individualism, the agrarian's faith and trust in constitutional political exchanges created a shared sense of civic obligation, while market exchanges, under Madison's rules, can be obtained in an orderly manner, without the benefit of shared faith or obligation to obey the rule of law.

From the view point of natural rights, market exchanges are not the moral equivalent of political exchanges, because market exchanges do not create bonds that tie together disassociated individuals in a cooperative society.

Part of Madison's unfair rules that applied directly to farmers trying to get away from the debt-lien system is that an orderly system of market exchanges substitutes special interest greed in exploiting government as the basis of binding individuals to the system of authority whose major dynamic is competitive special interest exploitation of the rules.

In the rules of Madison's elitist system, elites meet in private to negotiate over how laws and public resources should be used to further the special interests.

This process of meeting in secret is exactly the process followed by the 51 elites who met in secret in Philadelphia to negotiate the rules to overthrow the Articles of Confederation.

Political parties, comprised and controlled by special interest coalitions, use the apparatus of the party, such as precinct meetings, to mobilize blocks of voters to vote for candidates who will implement the details of the secret negotiations, once elected.

In this model of political decision making, there is no practical purpose served by having the political party attempt to translate the consent of the governed into law, because the governed and their consent, are not parties to the secret negotiations.

When the farmers were treated like any other special interest group, whose leaders entered into the secret negotiations about the public purpose, the farmers could see that the welfare outcomes were no different with their new party than it had been with their allegiance to the Democrats.

The paradox is that the agrarians believed that the American society was based upon a cultural emphasis on individual freedom. The agrarians added to that cultural emphasis their own belief in God's intervention in directing the affairs of the nation.

The addition of God allowed the agrarians to understand that the welfare of another individual is relevant to public policy deliberations. An agrarian leader in 1887 said, "God never intended His world be given over to the control and enjoyment of only a few individuals."

That translation from individual self interest to the public interest occurs as a result of the individual's mental ability to imagine improvements in the other's welfare and freedom.

The mistake that the agrarians made in the 1880s was in assuming that the elites shared this cultural emphasis and shared their ideas about God.

Just like today, when cultural conservatives continue to make the mistake that socialists are just like them in embracing the rule of law.

As Madison's special interest system evolved, the absence of mental values that reflect the welfare of another meant that both political parties became more and more self-oriented to promoting the interests of elites and more and more insulated from the concerns of ordinary Americans.

Citizens, in their role of voters, serve only to ratify the selection of candidates selected by the elite special interests.

This model is much like the political model that existed in the former Soviet empire, where the candidates for the Politburo were selected by communist party elites.

Madison understood, according to Marvin Meyers, in The Mind of the Founder, that man was a "social" animal moved by self-interest. His dilemma was how to re-write the rules of the Articles of Confederation so that "...self-interested, self-governing men would be obliged to respect the rights of others and serve the permanent and aggregate interests of the community."

What Meyers should have said, is that in the mind of the Founder, the issue related to how the elites could game the system so that non-elites respected the rights of the elites to serve their own elite interests.

In Federalist Paper number 57, Madison and Hamilton wrote that the most important barriers to the elevation of traitors to the public liberty were frequent elections and a "limitation of the term of appointments."

They discussed the issue of traitors to the public liberty in the context of corruption resulting from the private benefit gained from government resources. Aristotle called this concept of corruption self-aggrandizement from the use of public assets.

This type of corruption is evident in how Hillary gamed the system, with her fake charity. Hillary sold access to the American government to foreign countries, for the purpose of "self-aggrandizement."

The corruption discussed by Madison and Hamilton is different than the corruption identified by Aristotle. For Madison the real problem of corruption was government agents and representatives lying.

A better example of what Madison was worried about was the type of corruption of Obama continuously lying to the American public about his intentions to impose a socialist regime.

In Madison's conception of "traitor" Obama would be designated a traitor because he continually lied to the American public. Madison was primarily concerned about the consequences of elites lying to each other about economic exchanges, not about how the lies affected non-elites.

From the agrarian individual freedom perspective, an individual relies upon the trustworthiness of another to make decisions about the path of that individual's sovereignty.

If the information and data received from the government is false, then the individual decisions about sovereignty are flawed. Individuals enter the constitutional relationship with the presumption that the apparatus of government will provide stability and certainty to life's decisions because the government is a truthful agent.

Truth and trust, according to the agrarian interpretation of constitutional rules, have an entirely different meaning than Madison's interpretation. The agrarians never made this connection. They kept repeating their complaint, over and over again, that the rules were not fair.

If the special interests can achieve a united national culture of corruption, and if the elites can control the election apparatus in each district, with no fear of term limits, it does not matter from which district the elite is elected.

Once the elected representative arrives in Washington, D.C., the national values of the special interest corruption are all the same. Just like the values of the members of the Politburo are all the same once they arrive in Moscow.

The anti-federalists, in 1788, argued that the all-powerful central government created by Madison's constitution, would undermine both individual freedom and the power of local government. The anti-federalists, and even John Adams, predicted that Madison's rules would end in a corrupt tyranny.

Hamilton, for example, thought that the national bank, and the national debt would serve to bind the loyalty of the financial elite to protecting the national sovereignty.

Hamilton suggested that a national debt could become a "national blessing," because of its eventual use to perpetuate the special interest political system. But, in order to become a national blessing to the financial elites, the bank's burden of debt must be shifted to the backs on non-elites.

This is the reason that Hamilton led his army of 15,000 soldiers into western Pennsylvania, in 1794, to crush the farmers. The farmers were not living up to their side of the political bargain to pay their taxes, in gold.

By making the private financial interests of bankers compatible with the financial interests of the new nation, Hamilton could see a way to stabilize the fluctuating financial fortunes of the nation.

As written by Wilenz, "Hamilton's fiscal plan would, he believed, ally the federal government to a particular class of speculators, create (through the national bank) a means to dispense political bounties to political favorites and bribes to opponents and introduce what Madison would later describe as the "corrupt influence" of substituting the motive of private interests in place of the public duty."

As a result of this constitutional orientation, the role of the national government in economic policy matters became skewed towards issues like making certain that the bondholders of national debt were repaid at full face value for the bonds they had bought for pennies on the dollar.

As described by C. Vann Woodward, in Origins of The New South, "In their attack on the national banking system, the agrarian economists were on solid ground in contending that private privilege was exercising a sovereign power, a power of regulating national currency, for private gain rather than for meeting the needs of the country."

A private special interest exercising a sovereign political power, however, is the logical conclusion of Madison's constitutional system.

As an added bonus for the elites, Madison's unfair rules allowed the elites to take the farmer's lands when they did not pay their taxes, in gold and silver.

Bruce Palmer, in Man Over Money: The Southern Populist Critique of American Capitalism, noted that from 1865 to 1900, 50% of all farmers in the South had lost title to their land through the crop-lien system.

It was not simply the debt-lien laws that the farmers found so unfair. Beginning in the 1880's, the Democrats in the South passed a series of "anti-enticement laws" that made it illegal to entice a farmer from the land of his Landlord, or to "aid or abet" the farmer in transportation from the land.

As noted by Wood, the combination of laws, "allowed the planters to create a labor force whose freedom was severely curtailed by the indebtedness arising from the operation of the lien system and reinforced by the actions of the State."

By virtue of their debt-peonage system of taking the land from the farmers, the elite now were land-rich and needed the government to help them convert their land to cash.

Converting their land wealth to money involved an entirely different set of laws to benefit the elite.

The stability of the system, for the elites, as the farmers figured out in 1898, was more important than the fairness of the system of justice meted out to the farmers in the debt-lien system, and subsequently in the neo-slavery system of the cotton mills.

Paul Escott quotes a farmer, J. A. Wilson, from Mecklinburg County, N. C., speaking in 1894, "Owing to legislation in favor of monopolies, our lands are gradually slipping away from the hands of the wealth-producing classes and going into the hands of the few."

In other words, the agrarians could see what was happening to their lives as a result of the unfair rules, but they never understood that the elites did not share their starting assumptions about morality and justice.

The agrarians would have been much better off to re-examine the initial principles of Jefferson and worked towards a new constitution that aimed at equal rights for all, and special privileges for none. That same advice applies to conservatives in America today, who continue to believe that the socialists are just like conservatives in their allegiance to the rule of law.

Chapter 3.
The Agrarian Interpretation of Individual Morality In an Individualistic Equal Rights Society

One of the "truths" that Jefferson stated in the Declaration to be self-evident, was the truth that individuals were endowed by their Creator with certain inalienable rights. Not only did citizens have rights, but that the rights were held by Jefferson to be "self-evident" to all citizens.

As Micheal Zuckert described it in The Natural Rights Republic, to be an American means accepting the universal truths contained in the Declaration of Independence. Those truths were held, by Jefferson, to be self-evident, meaning outside of a chain of logic, and not derived from any other propositions.

They are held, Zuckert noted as, "...self-evident within the political community dedicated to making them effective."

The agrarians deeply believed in the truth of this proposition. They thought that God had granted them certain natural rights, and they believed in the equality that all Americans shared these rights. If they could see these rights as self-evident, then the agrarians thought that all Americans could also see these rights, and that all Americans accepted the universal truth of the proposition.

The agrarians belief system was intuitively obvious to them. There is also a biological scientific basis for their intuitive belief about individual rights. The scientific explanation involves how the hum brain searches and sorts images to come up with a plan of success and survival.

The human brain is continually sorting and selecting images in an attempt to organize a coherent picture of the individual's inner mental life mission. This activity in the brain would go on no matter what type of ambient cultural values or constitutional rules existed.

The brain is continually testing the internal mental images against external images in an attempt to find a degree of truthful representation. In very broad terms, the brain in engaged in the creation and re-creation of the mental model of the self, in an attempt to come up with strategies that allow some control over one's destiny, or life mission.

The brain's ability to spin out insights and images is the defining characteristic of the word "individual."

The insight/imagination function of the brain, which evolved from five million years of trial and error in random variation and natural selection, generates a completely unique mental world of each individual.

The mental world of one individual, at any single point in time, is different from another individual, even if the external event being viewed is the same.

The biological purpose served by the insight/imagination function is to give the individual the best alternative to choose from in deciding the course of behavior that promotes the sovereignty of the individual.

A collectivist society is always denying the individual the urge for this biologically defined sovereignty. Socialism denies this reality because for socialist all truth is relative.

Michael Gazzaniga, in his book, Nature's Mind: The Biological Roots of Thinking, makes a similar point about the ability of all citizens to see the truth of the proposition.

He wrote, "Clearly, the brain mechanism that allows for the "feeling of control" is one that has considerable survival power...society must examine the social programs, policies, and institutions that, although established [by government] to provide and care for us, actually minimize our influence over our environment."

The context of Gazzaniga's writing was the collectivist, liberal welfare state policies that ultimately leads to individual subjugation to the elite, and loss of control over individual freedom of choice in life's mission.

The agrarians assumed that all Americans shared a unique set of common mental images of trust and truth that led them back to the initial rules about how individuals should treat each other. They obtained this idea from reading Jefferson's Declaration.

The public purpose behind the formation of Jefferson's Declaration and the nation's first constitution was to allow individuals to make decisions about their own sovereign life mission.,

The integrity of the collective decision making process is promoted when truth is elevated above other ordinary civil or economic transactions. This collective good reinforces the public purpose of individual freedom, which, as described in the passage above, constitutes the motivational premise individuals have for leaving the state of nature and entering a constitutional relationship.

The elevation of truth to the level of constitutional deliberations, as opposed to the more every day considerations of civil disputes between individuals, affects the level and severity of punishment when constitutional prohibitions against lying are violated.

If public trust and public truth are relegated to the same status as a civil dispute involving economic transactions in the marketplace, then the same judicial forums for adjudicating both types of transgressions will be used.

Individual welfare, from a biological perspective, is improved when an individual can make decisions over their sovereignty and control their destiny. This is the function for which the brain is continually spinning out images and alternatives.

Individual welfare, from a political perspective, is not improved by having someone else, or some set of elites, determine the end state, or welfare outcome, for the individual.

Whether this unique constellation of cultural values is widespread and commonly-held throughout the society is contingent upon the process of social consensus about moral values.

As Mackie points out, societies are capable of creating values, but the adoption of one set of values versus some competing set of values depends on who controls the flow of information in society.

There are no formal rules of civil procedure, such as majority voting in an election, that determines which set of ambient cultural values becomes dominant in a specific society.

The public purpose in an individualist society is served by promotion and adherence to common external values of trust, fair dealing, truthful representations, and promise keeping.

Cooperation between individuals occurs when the individuals assume, prior to entering into the rights exchange process, that these common values are influencing the other brain's interpretation of truth the same way in both brains.

One reason why the agrarians kept referring to their supply buying markets as a "cooperative" is that they believed that individuals who shared common cultural values, like farmers, would "cooperate."

Following social civil rules has an effect on the development of individual morality which acts to secure voluntary obedience to the rules.

For Jefferson, the public purpose of freedom is served, and the glue that holds the democratic republican society together, is each individual's priority in having economic control over their life's destiny. Each individual depends upon the other to follow the civil rules of justice.

Under one unique set of cultural values regarding individual sovereignty, the public purpose is related to how and why the brain performs the insight/imagination function.

The logic of this argument, in other words, is that the biological function of the individual brain provides the rationale for why and how society should define the public purpose in terms of improving individual welfare.

The role of society should be to extend and enhance the individual's own biologically designed pursuit of sovereignty. The linkage between an individual's brain sorting images and the public purpose arises in the context of political exchanges with another individual.

In this context of exchange, the internal mental world of one individual is related to the internal mental world of another individual through shared external values created and perpetuated by the ambient culture.

A shared set of values about trust within a culture strengthens the degree of social cooperation. The shared values makes it more likely that individual brains will be sorting and selecting images based upon the coherence between internal models and external images during the course of an exchange.

Both individual and social cooperation occur when individual brains see the same external truths related to the value of trust. The images being sorted in one brain rely on the ambient values to inform the decision that trust extended to the other individual will be reciprocated.

This dependency on another to follow rules establishes the condition of welfare interdependency. Interdependent welfare functions arise as a result of both individuals following the rules of justice.

Allowing individuals the greatest freedom to pursue their destiny is the only unambiguous constitutional public purpose that would bind every individual to serving the public purpose. Serving the public purpose provides the logical justification for establishing the priority of individual welfare as the key unit of analysis in the political system that ensues from the constitutional framework.

In the individualist society, the role of government is to reduce the chance situations that other individuals, or the police power of the state, will be used to override the individual's freedoms of choice in pursuing their sovereign life mission.

The government serves this function by administering a framework of collective decision making whose goal is to secure just outcomes to the laws that individuals give to themselves. Government, and the pursuit of just outcomes, is a process, not an outcome.

The exclusive focus of the public purpose in Jefferson's framework of decision making is the individual's control over the life's mission. The public purpose is not on the wealth of nations, the welfare of groups, or the equal distribution of incomes that conform to a collectivist vision of fairness.

The essential, primary function of government in an individualistic society is to enforce a constant system of justice derived from rules that citizens give to themselves. The teleos of the system of justice is to reduce the arbitrary and capricious application of the rules of justice.

Consciousness is an internal state of the brain that facilitates a deliberative, rational process of making decisions about behavior. The conscious thought process is deliberative because the individual brain is sorting and selecting some images for further processing, and deliberately rejecting other images.

It is rational because the images that are being selected for further processing are targeted to achieving the specific goal of self-interest.

The process of "seeing the necessary truth," or "seeking for hope," involves imagining the possible outcomes of an exchange and feeling how that outcome affects the individual. Images and the imagination of outcomes are sorted and selected based upon how the different potential outcomes feel emotionally.

When the images ring true, or feel right, the neurons across all regions of the brain have lined up, and the internal mental world has reached a state of truth regarding the external images.

The pursuit of self interest through the rational decision making, truth-seeking, image-sorting function of the brain is, to borrow a phrase from computer engineering, hard-wired in the neuronal networks of the brain.

What is not hard-wired is the element of uncertainty associated with trust that the other individual will reciprocate in the social exchange or transaction. This element of uncertainty is one of the major images being sorted for truth.

The brain is aiming at the correct level of trust to extend to the other individual during the course of the exchange.

This deliberative, rational thinking process requires the individual to adopt the "on-looker" objective mental stance discussed earlier. The on-looker mental perspective allows the individual an opportunity to try out, imaginatively, the different outcomes.

The on-looker stance requires that the individual suspend, for extended periods of time, the current emotional state and feelings, in order to try out the imagined outcomes. Daniel Dennett describes this insight-imagination function of the brain as swiftly producing the future.

The propensity of any individual to obey social rules in any given exchange is determined by how strongly that individual adheres to the cultural values of mutual obligation and mutual reciprocity.

As John Eccles notes in his book, Evolution of the Brain: Creation of the Self "...the brain is built with the propensity for performance according to value systems, and the value system initially learned is that of the ambient culture."

In other words, the propensity to obey social rules is a function of both the individual's own internal value system, which is further reinforced by the values in the ambient culture. Whether an individual will obey social rules is contingent upon on how strongly the ambient culture emphasizes the values of obligation and reciprocity in exchanges.

The issue of the uncertainty of rule adherence highlights the importance in a democratic republic of the "rule of law" as applied to all individuals once the constitution has been created. The equal application of the rule of law however requires an institutional framework through which the application can be applied.

If the institutions are designed to adjudicate rights, then the rule of law can be applied uniformly. If, on the other hand, institutions were conceived in the initial constitution as the mechanism to separate and balance political powers, then rights adjudication becomes more uncertain, contributing to the social uncertainty about rule adherence.

In conditions of uncertainty over future obligations which leads to short term calculative behavior, the political institutions themselves become targets of social control for facilitating short term political behavior.

Short term private advantage, gained through rule breaking and manipulation, comes at the cost of mental dissonance between one's own truth about the sovereign self, and the reality being filtered in the brains of other individuals.

The mental dissonance of rule breaking makes the brain's filtering process less certain about the path of sovereignty to follow because the rule-breaker is never certain of future reciprocity in value exchanges with others.

Jefferson's original purpose of codifying constitutional rules was to provide for greater certainty for the individual to gain control over his or her life's mission. Rule breaking undermines this original purpose.

Madison overthrew Jefferson's public purpose, and failed to substitute any force that would compel voluntary compliance with constitutional rules.

It is within this context of individualism that Mackie's suggestion can be applied to the question raised by the agrarians about how one's interest for his or her life's mission to be consistent with the public purpose.

In Man Over Money: The Southern Populist Critique of American Capitalism, Bruce Palmer, noted that the agrarians believed in "the right of the people to govern themselves…that government is not something separate from the people, but simply the people governing themselves."

J. L. Mackie, in Ethics: Inventing Right and Wrong, asked the same question that was continually raised by the agrarians about why the elites did not share the truth of this proposition. The agrarians asked this same question over and over again, always in a state of disbelief about the non-shared values, that were so self-evident in the Declaration.

In a society based upon equal individual rights, the agrarians asked, what type of person is it in my interest to be? And, if I can imagine what type of person I should be, do I have the political power to become that person?

Mackie goes on to outline the idea that society and cultural values, such as the idea of ethical values, are creations of society. Mackie suggests that the individual's life mission should be consistent with the public good, when the public good means cooperation in the pursuit of individual sovereignty. His suggestion implies a culturally specific definition of the term "individual," and a culturally specific relationship to social ethical values.

Madison got this part wrong. Madison thought that only the elite had virtue and morality.

In contrast to Madison, the agrarians believed that individuals are connected to each other through the external values of truth and trust because these values influence the way each individual's brain processes the truth.

In the individualistic society of equal rights for all, all brains are equal and rational in processing the sovereign life path of the individual.

Mackie's suggestion about the invention of ethical social rules means that there is a unique constellation of ethical values and institutional arrangements in politics and economics that define the pursuit of the public purpose from an individualist value orientation.

When this set of cultural values and institutional arrangements are in place, obedience to social rules and laws does not require a King, or Church, or a Leviathan, or the coercive power of the socialist state.

An individual citizen's morality is derived from interdependent welfare functions, or mental images in the citizen's brain that concern the welfare of another citizen.

In other words, morality in future obligations in a social exchange leads back, ultimately, to the agrarian's awareness of God. An individual's mental image of God can not be subjected to enforcement by the collective police power of the state without destroying the essence of the individual.

In the individualist society, the moral freedom of the individual is the teleos, or goal to which the society is directed. This teleos involves the decreasing reliance on externally imposed standards of behavior and ethical values regarding the treatment of others in civil exchanges.

Moral development of the individual occurs during life through an increasing reliance on internalized mental values that address the welfare of others. This moral development process occurs when individuals have the greatest freedom of choice over their mental images, and the greatest control over the choice in pursuing their own sovereign life mission.

Under collectivism and socialism, it is the socialist elites who define morality, not the individual.

In the Roots of Southern Populism, Steven Hahn summarizes the differences in philosophy between the agrarians and the elites. First, the agrarians understood that the increasing wealth and economic power in the market place was transferring a certain range of political privileges from economic affairs to political affairs.

That transfer of economic power translated into a political ability to exercise sovereign political power over farmers that was not in any way derived from the consent of the governed, and was not subject to reform through the mechanism of electoral politics.

The political power of the elites drew its sustenance from economic power, and was concentrated in the branches of the federal government, making local and state governments less able to ameliorate the effects of the elite's power and privileges.

The concentrated elite political power subjugated each farmer's interests to the interests of the elite. In other words, the farmer's no longer had the ability to pursue life, liberty, or happiness.

Free market economic exchange relies on the market pricing mechanism to coordinate voluntary behavior of autonomous, sovereign individuals in the current unit of time.

The theoretical problem is that free market exchange, when transferred to Madison's constitutional setting for political rules, involves power and fate control of the elites over the non-elites, which requires the imposition of the police power to enforce obligation to the rules of economic exchange.

In an elitist, or collectivist society, only a small segment of the brains are thought to be capable of making the rational decisions about what is in one's best interest.

In contrast to social rights exchange outlined in the Declaration, Madison's constitutional economic exchanges are based upon power relationships involving fate control between elites and non-elites.

For the agrarians, the unit of exchange was trust between individuals. For Madison, the unit of exchange was money.

The value of trust in social political exchanges and the value of money in Madison's economic exchanges overlap.

The definition of the individual in collectivist cultures rules out the uniqueness of each individual's truth processing, and substitutes for it group processing of truth. In a collectivist society, the development of the individual moral personality is overridden by the imposition of the collectivist morality, which always overrides individual sovereignty.

In other words, the extension of trust is an act of faith in the sense that the individual assumes, during the course of the exchange, that the other brain is seeing the same external values, and is being influenced by those values.

The agrarians thought that in all political exchanges involving individual freedom, that the constitution provided the mechanism through which the act of faith is reciprocated.

Isaiah Berlin, in The Crooked Timber of Humanity, argues for limiting the power of institutions to performing a select set of functions.

In order to avoid damaging individual sovereignty, Berlin suggests that "...it would follow that the creation of a social structure that would, at best, avoid morally intolerable alternatives, and at the most promote active solidarity in the pursuit of common objectives may be the best that human beings can be expected to achieve, if too many varieties of positive action are not to be repressed, to many equally valid human goals are not to be frustrated."

The agrarians never gave up on their beliefs that the elites shared their cultural values about individual freedom, even when it became evident to the agrarians that there was a fundamental disconnect between their beliefs and the beliefs of the elites about equal rights for all.

This interpretation of the Populist belief in shared values was given by Carl Degler, in The Other South, who wrote, "The Populists did not object to the (free market) system; they merely wanted a fair chance to prosper under it. They had been lead to believe...that America was the home of opportunity."

Writing in Progressive Farmer, the magazine that he founded, Leonidas Polk wrote "We do not wish to be rich but only want a reasonable chance that we may be able to achieve decent and respectable lives and educate our children. Surely no enemy could say anything against such a doctrine as this."

It is much easier to maintain control of social decision making when non-elites become dependent upon the elites for welfare, and when non-elites are consequently stripped of their natural biological urge to seek control over their destiny.

It would be much harder for the elites to maintain political power over thousands of independent-minded citizens making hundreds of thousands of autonomous mental decisions about their own welfare and futures.

Furthermore, welfare-dependent non-elites, who do not rely upon individual initiative to fulfill their own life's destiny, do not need to make, during their brain's image sorting and filtering processes, decisions that incorporate the welfare of others.

The natural evolutionary mental decision process about one's own welfare that eventually leads to individual morality is short-circuited in Madison's rules. In order for Madison's rules of procedure for a representative republic to work, without becoming totalitarian, he needed to make a clear distinction in his constitution between private and public good.

Government can not be conceived as the engine for all good because the government does not have the ability to "imagine" or visualize an intrinsic definition of the common good.

Once agents of government in Madison's system escaped from their leash of the consent of the governed, his system became less a republic, and more like a private corporation, with a latent potential for totalitarianism.

Periodically changing the board of directors of the corporation does not change the underlying ends of the corporation, which is to keep the status quo arrangement of power in place to distribute benefits to the special interests.

In place of Jefferson's faith in individual morality, the elites substitute a totalitarian set of politically correct values, as determined by the elite, that tell non-elites how to react to unknown circumstances and questions that involve the welfare of others.

The most damaging aspect of this value substitution in America today is the effect on individual freedom and the related effect on individual morality.

There must be a set of certain required minimum, nascent conditions in the ambient culture to allow some minimal level of shared constitutional values about morality and truth to be exchanged.

Madison's constitution did not contain the set of shared values about morality and truth. The Declaration and The Articles of Confederation did contain these values.

The agrarians mistakenly assumed that the values of the Declaration had been transferred to Madison's constitution, and assumed that all Americans shared this set of values about freedom and truth, as being "self-evident."

The elite Federalists, however, did not conceive of the American society as comprised of individuals. Rather, Madison imposed the British class structure on the American society to provide the elites with an enduring special advantage and privilege.

The agrarians never understood this part about Madison's rules of procedure.

The agrarians would have done so much better if they had jettisoned Madison's value-free constitutional rules in favor of creating fair rules based upon their motto: Equal rights for all. Special privileges for none.

Chapter 4.
Rational Choice in An Individualistic Decentralized American Government

The agrarian's desire for better welfare outcomes for each individual, based upon a public purpose of individual freedom, must start the investigation for better constitutional rules at the point where the self-evident cultural values in the Declaration influence individual's morality to obey the rules.

The purpose of the investigation is not exclusively to secure obedience to existing social rules of justice, but to allow for the creation of rules where each individual gains maximum control over his or her own fate through interdependent welfare exchanges that are governed by morality.

The goal of the new constitution is to outline the rules of procedure that allow citizens to translate their preferences into law. If the citizens have this power, then the logic of self-government is that the citizens will voluntarily obey they rules that they make for themselves.

In leaving the state of nature, and forming a constitution, individuals are placed in a position of uncertainty in the outcome of their life's mission. No individual knows in advance where the individual may end up, given the choice between one set of constitutional rules or another.

A rational individual, with a rational self-interest, would choose fair rules for all, aimed at the greatest freedom for all. In constitutional decision-making under uncertainty, individuals would seek rules that had maximum equal rights for all, with special privileges for none.

The end goal, or teleos, of the constitution, in this case of rational self-interest, is individual freedom.

In Constitutional Economics, James Buchanan relies on a philosophy of logic to explain how the end goals, clearly stated in a constitution, create the binding allegiance to follow rules.

"Uncertainty about just where one's own interest will lie in a sequence of plays or rounds will lead a rational person, from his own interest, to prefer rules and arrangements, or constitutions that will seem fair, no matter what final positions he might occupy."

In other words, rather than relying on the separation of powers between social classes to deal with the problem of self-interest corruption, as Madison did, Buchanan relies upon the rationality of self-interest as a force that binds individuals to society as a process of rationally minimizing risk in uncertain decision making environments.

Buchanan and Geoffrey Brennan emphasized that the development of fair rules is a political process, in contrast to the current political system's emphasis of allowing government agents to achieve a desired welfare outcome in the distribution of income among social groups.

In The Reason of Rules, they write that,

> *"Our specific claim is that justice takes its meaning from the rules for the social order within which notions of justice are to be applied. To appeal to considerations of justice is to appeal to relevant rules."*

This interpretation of justice as fair rules is dramatically different than the socialist Rawlsian notion that relies on a set of elites who judge the fairness of welfare outcomes, and have the power to shift resources from one social group to another.

Buchanan continues by noting,

> *"To the extent that this (existing American) constitution commands little respect, in part because it is seen to fail in its function of limiting the scope of both governmental and private intrusion into what are widely held to be protected spheres of activity."*

Madison's constitution allows the central government to operate directly upon the citizens without providing the mechanism for citizens to operate directly on the central government.

It is this direct operation of centralized power on citizen freedoms that constitutes the greatest threat, if socialists ever obtain the reins of centralized power.

As Sean Wilentz wrote, in The Rise of American Democracy: Jefferson to Lincoln, in Madison's rules,

"The people had no formal voice of their own in government. And, that was exactly how it was supposed to be – for once the electors had chosen their representatives, they ceded power, reserving none for themselves until the next election…The people, as a political entity, existed only on election day."

Madison's arrangement reserved no powers to the citizens, and the result is a special interest tyranny that operates on behalf of the natural aristocracy.

In a socialist dictatorship, not only would the socialist elites plunder the wealth, but they would impose their mentally deranged religious views of fairness on the citizens.

Brennan and Buchanan's remedy for the special interest tyranny is on the potential for changes in the constitutional rules. "These rules," they note, "provide the framework within which patterns of distributional end states emerge from the interaction of persons who play various complex functional roles."

Their entire constitutional edifice is based upon rational individual choice and decision making.

In his book, The Theory of Public Choice, II, Buchanan defines an individual not so much from the perspective of the brain's insight-imagination, but from the brain's rational choice attribute.

He states, that

> "...we can simply define a person in terms of his set of preferences, his utility function. This function defines or describes a set of possible trade-offs among alternatives for potential choice."

While Buchanan's initial definition identifies the brain's rational choice function in terms of self-interest, he later ties the self-interest back to rule obedience that results from an awareness of the welfare of another individual by suggesting the possibility of an interdependent utility function.

For Buchanan, the free market exchange system provides an instrumental value of freedom by creating the means of escape from coercion, exploitation, and subjugation.

Buchanan makes a clean distinction between the constitutional rules that govern economic exchanges, and those constitutional rules that define moral relationships between individuals.

Free market exchanges would become a means to facilitate individual freedom, not a public end in and of itself.

Morality in market exchanges would become an issue of public concern whenever fate control involving coercion, manipulation and subjugation occurred. This outcome of subjugation is precisely the point that the agrarians were making about their unfair status.

The farmers were being subjugated to the interests of the bankers and merchants, but the farmers did not have a constitutional right to remedy the abuse, under Madison's rules.

The farmers had no means of escape from the coercive exchange relationships with the bankers.

Buchanan, in Constitutional Economics, described that elected representatives, once they get to the nation's capital, adopt a welfare function that is different from the welfare function of the citizens that they purport to represent.

In Madison's special interest rules, the welfare function that politicians maximize is their own individual function. Partisan gain, viewed from the perspective of the individual politician, is gain that benefits the politician.

In Buchanan's conception, there is no logical rule making mechanism to prohibit the elected representative from substituting the maximization of their own welfare function, as a part of imagining the improvement of social group welfare.

Once a centralized government bureaucracy is created that is removed from the consent of the governed, the bureaucracy develops its own interpretation of the social welfare function it presumes to maximize.

If the bureaucracy was originally created to serve the needs of a special interest group, then that group's special interest preferences become the surrogate social welfare function.

As Buchanan has pointed out, that surrogate social welfare function contains variables that promote the welfare of the politicians and bureaucrats who created it.

The welfare function they maximize turns out to be their own. If it is not subjected to sunset or recall, the bureaucracy becomes a permanent feature of the political infrastructure.

In its more general application, Arrow's impossibility theorem predicts that tyranny, not majority rule democracy, is the general rule making mechanism of the special interest political system.

Buchanan addressed how to solve this question in his book The Theory of Public Choice, II, when he described the difference between "economic man," and "moral man."

Economic man, according to Buchanan, is defined by his utility function, whose variables are weighted according to their contribution to monetary wealth.

"His behavior," notes Buchanan, "in the economic relationship is not influenced by ethical or moral considerations that serve to constrain his pursuit of his objectively defined interest."

The mistake that the agrarians made, over and over again, in their complaint about fair outcomes, is that they never understood that the bankers and merchants were acting as economic men, not moral men.

The agrarians, on the other hand, were acting as moral men, because that is how they understood what Jefferson was saying in the Declaration, about self-evident rights.

The agrarians complaint never obtained a just outcome because the elites who ruled them were not then, and are not now, influenced by ethical or moral considerations.

Madison had set up the initial rules to favor the elites because, he falsely argued, that the elites were "virtuous." Once in operation, Madison's rules allowed the elites to act beyond the rule of law because there are no consequences for them in obeying the rule of law.

Under Madison's constitutional rules, market exchanges are the supreme social values, and investment decisions, which partially determine both prices and justice, are left to the private investment decisions of elites.

The absence of morality in economic exchanges necessitates the deployment of the police power of the state to enforce the terms and conditions of the economic exchange contract.

Distribution of equal benefit to individuals of equal merit is not currently possible in Madison's constitutional government because fairness requires an independent objective panel of judges to determine equal merit.

Part of the threat to liberty in contemporary politics is that the socialist elites believe that they are the only citizens worthy of being the judges of fairness.

In Madison's rules, the rule of law, and the coercive police power of the state to enforce the law, the law is for the "little people." The rule of law applies to the laws passed by the elites to extract benefits from the non-elites and to enforce subjugation on the non-elites.

In a contemporary example of Aristotle's corruption, Hillary is beyond the rule of law. Obama is beyond the rule of law. In Madison's conception of rights, laws made by the elites apply to the non-elites.

In contrast to Madison, Buchanan argues that the voluntary compliance with the rule of law, based upon moral reciprocity in the constitution, leads to rule obedience because all citizens are subject to the uncertainty that they may, one day, find themselves at the bottom of the economic totem pole.

In other words, human rational choice leads to voluntary constitutional rule obedience, under Buchanan's rules. Rule obedience, in the free market system, leads to the fair economic outcomes that the agrarians so desperately wanted to obtain.

Free market exchanges would become a means to facilitate individual freedom, not a public end in and of itself. Morality in market exchanges would become an issue of public concern whenever fate control involving coercion, manipulation and subjugation occurred.

The public interest priority would be especially high in cases of market exchange where one individual has no means of escape from the exchange relationship.

The farmers, for example, did not have a means of escape from the debt-lien system.

The moral value of the market exchange system lies in its ability to create opportunities for the individual to fulfill his destiny. That path of sovereignty for the individual is the same for all individuals.

In other words, it is a constitutional system based upon equal rights for all and special privileges for none.

Chapter 5.
The Rationale of the Federalist Centralization of Government Power

There was nothing wrong with the functioning, or the administrative procedures employed, under the Articles of Confederation. Many of the anti-federalists made this argument in 1788, during the ratification debates.

The agrarians, of 1888, kept looking back in history and imagining that the unfair rules they labored under were still the rules of the Articles, because the agrarians still believed that the principles of self-government contained in Jefferson's Declaration were still in effect.

The agrarian arguments about fairness, in 1888, were based upon this mistake. The Declaration had not been overtly revoked by the Federalists, but the Articles of Confederation had been revoked, and replaced by constitutional rules that ignored the principles of self-government.

The Federalists engaged in a massive propaganda campaign to impose their fraudulent scheme on the farmers. Their propaganda included using the U. S. Postal system as a weapon to limit communication between anti-federalists, media distortion of the anti-federalist arguments, voter fraud in state ratification elections, and violence to prohibit anti-federalists from engaging in legitimate debate.

That propaganda continues today under the guise of academic historians who continue to celebrate the brilliance of the Federalist scheme.

The common term used by academic scholars to describe the 51 elites who met in secret, in 1787, to overthrow a constitutional government is "Founding Fathers."

From the viewpoint of the elites, what was wrong with Jefferson's notions about equality, and what was wrong with the rules of the Articles, was that the rules allowed the farmer's to pay their taxes in paper money.

The states, under the authority granted to them in the Articles, had passed laws that allowed the states to issue paper money that was considered "legal tender." Legal tender means that the paper money had to be accepted in all financial exchanges, both within a state's borders, and in the other states.

The elites, who owned most of the bonds that had financed the Revolution, wanted their interest payments to be made in gold and silver, not in paper money. Gold and silver currency, however, did not exist in circulation for the farmers to pay their taxes.

Ergo, the Federalists met in Philadelphia to eviscerate the power of the states to issue paper money, and replaced both local and state government with a coercive centralized government.

Madison's scheme deployed the British social class system of government, based upon his idea of two social classes. In the mind of the Founder, there were "the well-born," and there were the "masses."

Or, as Hamilton was fond of calling them, "the howling masses."

The howling masses were unfit to govern because as soon as they had the authority to govern, at the state level, the masses enacted tyrannical democratic rules that allowed farmers to pay their taxes in paper money.

Madison called these state laws "tyrannical" because the majority of voters (farmers) were using their majority votes to the disadvantage of the minority of bond-holders (elites).

The scheme imposed by the Federalists created an economic system that was predicated on land and bond speculation. The speculation by the elites created a wildly unstable macro economy in the United States that collapsed every 10 years, or so.

The most recent episode of speculation occurred in 2008, based upon land and bond speculation, controlled to benefit the elites. Except, by 2008, it was not just domestic U. S. elites who benefited from the speculation.

The system of speculation had evolved to include the financial elites of the world.

In 2009, a socialist was inaugurated as President, and assumed the centralized government's, global powers, that had been created by Madison.

The socialist spent the next eight years using the centralized power to promote his ideas of fairness, in a global socialist scheme. The next book, in this series, A Civil Dissolution, will describe why the socialism in America constitutes a clear and present danger to non-socialists.

For the agrarians of 1887, however, the elites had created an intolerable, unfair set of economic conditions. The outcome that the agrarians wanted was fair rules of exchange.

Jefferson provided some elaboration on his concept of decentralized self-government. As implemented in the Articles of Confederation, the rules would establish a priority of local and state governments over national governments based on the principle that those bound most tightly by collective rules must be given the greatest say in the making and enforcing of the rules.

In other words, Jefferson's idea of "consent of the governed" found its greatest application in local and state government, whose political authority would be superior to the national government.

This priority of local government over national government has a very subtle point about the application of Jefferson's principle of equality before the law.

If all individuals are equal in the making and enforcing of the law, and the law is applied most stringently at the most local level of the community, then no individual is greater than the law.

In order to promote the greatest level of individual freedom, all individuals must be bound, in equal capacity, by the same law that they have given to themselves.

In the cultural and social context of the agrarians, all citizens were equal, socially. The way that this idea was expressed by farmers in North Carolina was "you are no better than me, and I am no better than you."

Rule obedience and rule enforcement depend on shared values of equality being filtered and sorted in each brain of the individual who is a party to the contract, both during the time of the initial exchange, and in the post-exchange period, which may last indefinitely.

The agrarians first attempted reform at the state and local level of government because that was where the farmers found the most reciprocity in exchange of equal values.

The elites, however, were not bound by local laws, and did not share the values of equality of the farmers because they thought the farmers were "unfit."

The political elites of 1888 were not bound by the same rules that they imposed upon the non-elite, and not subjected to feelings of cultural value disloyalty when they manipulated the rules for their own advantage.

In contemporary times, Hillary does not believe that she is bound by the same rules as the non-elites, because Hillary thinks she is beyond the rule of law. Hillary is not an exception to this rule.

All socialists believe that they are beyond the rule of law, both because of their good intentions for imposing their rules on non-socialists, and their obvious intellectual superiority to make all political decisions.

The elites, in 1888, were acting in their capacity of "economic man," not moral man. The agrarians were acting in their political capacity as moral man, and thought that the elites shared their moral values.

Reciprocity in a market exchange is a matter of contract law that depends upon the constitutional structure. Reciprocity in the moral exchange is dependent on faith in that the other individual shares moral values.

Obedience to the institutional rules of justice in an individualistic society, meaning the judicial system, the economic system, and the system of political representation, all rest upon a very fragile foundation of faith that all brains are processing mental images of common cultural values.

Madison's system did not express any cultural values, and the elites of 1888 did not share the values of the farmers about fair outcomes in political or economic exchanges.

The agrarians never figured out this part about the elites, and never figured out that it was their allegiance to local and state government that provided them with the moral framework for justice.

Jefferson's principle that all legitimate power is derived directly from the consent of the governed relates to the control of the government apparatus in order that individual freedom may by protected, both from the tyranny of government agents, and from the external threat of foreign governments.

The farmer's held a deep, religious faith in this principle of the legitimate authority of government.

In other words, the farmers were trying to adopt fair rules of cooperation and competition, which would determine the distribution of income and opportunities.

The Populists captured the essence of this political orientation in their motto "Equal rights for all. Special Privileges for none."

That motto works effectively in a political system that aims at citizen participation in the development of fair rules.

The Federalist elites of 1788, the banking elites of 1888, and the socialists of 2008, all share an ideological antipathy towards individualism. Their ideology is based upon their belief of how important elites are to making the right type of collectivist decisions on behalf of disadvantaged groups.

The most important anti-federalist/agrarian cultural value is the value of maximum individual freedom.

As noted by Brennan and Buchanan, "Individuals are recognized to possess their own privately determined objectives, their own life plans, and these need not be common to all persons. In this setting, rules have the function of facilitating interactions among persons who may desire quite different things."

The great virtue of the competitive free market system is that voluntary, cooperative social behavior coordination can be achieved without tyranny and totalitarianism.

That entire voluntary, cooperative system though, depends, as Jefferson observed, on a belief and faith in individual's as their own best guardians of individual welfare.

The juncture of authority between individuals and government is the major point of conflict between collectivism and individualism.

Madison promised in Federalist #10 that "...the general government is not to be charged with the whole power of making and administering laws: its jurisdiction is limited to certain enumerated objects, which concern all members of the republic."

As noted by Meyers, in The Mind of the Founder, Madison went on to argue that the "powers delegated by the proposed constitution to the federal government are few and defined, exercised principally on external objects, as war, peace, negotiation, and foreign commerce..."

Madison's rules of procedure would have required an underpinning of individualism to prohibit the extension of federal power, but he personally did not trust common citizens to be their own best guardians.

Even though Madison made the same argument as Jefferson, that "It violates the vital principle of a free government that those that are to be bound by laws, ought to have a voice in making them," his system reserved the mass of sovereign power to the central government.

In their conception of power, Madison and Hamilton left no room for voluntary, free market coordination of behavior.

Forrest McDonald, in Novus Ordo Seclorum, made this point by quoting Hamilton, who said, "The powers of sovereignty are in this country divided between the National and State Governments and each of the portions of powers delegated to the one or the other is sovereign with regard to its proper power."

This statement by Hamilton is a political ruse and propaganda. He did not believe this statement to be true at the time he made it.

Once the reins of government were captured by the special interests, the operation of the market became another policy area to be manipulated.

There was no place in the rules for the farmers to implement Jefferson's confidence in the common citizen's ability to work out his own problems, free of government oversight and coercion.

The Federalist centralization of government power is irrational because it does not allow individuals to make rational decisions about their sovereign life path. No amount of tinkering with amendments is going to overcome the irrationality of Madison's constitution.

A better idea is to pick up where the farmers left off, and implement a new constitution based upon the principles of equal rights for all, special privileges for none.

BIBLIOGRAPHY

Adams, John, *The Political Writings of John Adams: Representative Selections*, Edited with an Introd. by George A. Peek, Jr., New York, Liberal Arts Press, 1954.

Arrow, Kenneth Joseph, *Social Choice and Individual Values*, New York, Wiley, 1951.

Ayers, Edward L., *The Promise of the New South: Life After Reconstruction*, New York, Oxford University Press, 1992.

Bass, Jack, and DeVries, Walter, *The Transformation of Southern Politics: Social Change and Political Consequence Since 1945*. Athens, University of Georgia Press, 1995.

Bassett, John Spencer, *Slavery in the State of North Carolina*, Baltimore, Johns Hopkins Press, 1899, New York, AMS Press, 1972.

Beard, Charles Austin, *The Economic Origins of Jeffersonian Democracy*, New York, Macmillan Co., 1915.

Berlin, Isaiah, Sir, *The Crooked Timber of Humanity: Chapters in the History of Ideas*, Edited by Henry Hardy, London, John Murray, 1990.

Billings, Dwight B., *Planters and the Making of a "New South": Class, Politics, and Development in North Carolina, 1865-1900*, Chapel Hill, University of North Carolina Press, 1979.

Blau, Peter Michael, *Exchange and Power in Social Life*, New York, J. Wiley, 1964.

Brennan, Geoffrey, and Buchanan, James M., *The Reason of Rules: Constitutional Political Economy*, Cambridge, New York, Cambridge University Press, 1985.

Buchanan, James M., *Constitutional Economics*, Oxford, UK., Cambridge, Mass., Blackwell, 1991.

Buchanan, James M., *Theory of Public Choice: Political Applications of Economics*, Ann Arbor, University of Michigan Press, 1972.

Busby, Josh, *Evolution of North Carolina's Economic Development*, Honors Essay: Dept. of Political Science, University of North Carolina at Chapel Hill, 1993.

Calvin, William H., <u>The Cerebral Symphony: Seashore Reflections on the Structure of Consciousness,</u> New York, Bantam Books, 1990.

Cash, W. J. (Wilbur Joseph), <u>The Mind of the South: 1900-1941,</u> 1st ed., New York, Alfred A. Knopf, 1941.

Cecil-Fronsman, Bill, <u>Common Whites: Class and Culture In Antebellum</u>, Lexington, KY., University Press of Kentucky, 1992.

Clayton, Bruce D., <u>The Savage Ideal: Intolerance and Intellectual Leadership in the South, 1890-1914,</u> Baltimore, Johns Hopkins University Press, 1972.

Coombs, Rod, Saviotti, Paolo, Walsh, Vivien, <u>Economics and Technological Change,</u> Basingstoke, Macmillan, 1987.

Crossan, John Dominic, <u>The Historical Jesus:. The Life of a Mediterranean Jewish Peasant,</u> 1st ed., San Francisco, Harper, 1991.

Degler, Carl N., <u>The Other South: Southern Dissenters in the Nineteenth Century,</u> 1st ed., New York, Harper & Row, 1974.

Dennett, Daniel Clement, <u>Consciousness Explained</u>, 1st ed., Boston, Little, Brown and Co., 1991.

Douglass, Elisha P., <u>Rebels and Democrats: The Struggle For Equal Political Rights and Majority Rule During the American Revolution</u>, Chapel Hill, University of North Carolina Press, 1955.

Eccles, John C., (John Carew), Sir, <u>Evolution of the Brain: Creation of the Self</u>, London, New York, Routledge, 1989.

Eliade, Mircea, <u>The Sacred and the Profane: The Nature of Religion</u>, 1st American ed., New York, Harcourt, Brace, 1959.

Escott, Paul D., <u>Many Excellent People: Power and Privilege in North Carolina, 1850-1900</u>, Chapel Hill, University of North Carolina Press, 1985.

Gazzaniga, Michael S., <u>Nature's Mind: The Biological Roots of Thinking, Emotions, Sexuality, Language and Intelligence,</u> New York, Basic Books, 1992.

Genovese, Eugene D., <u>The Slaveholders' Dilemma: Freedom and Progress in Southern Conservative Thought, 1820-1860,</u> Columbia, S.C., University of South Carolina Press, 1992.

Goldwin, Robert A., *From Parchment to Power: How James Madison Used the Bill of Rights to Save the Constitution,* Washington, DC, AEI Press, 1997.

Goodwyn, Lawrence. *Democratic Promise: The Populist Moment in America*, New York, Oxford University Press, 1976.

Granovetter, Mark and Swedberg, Richard, *The Sociology of Economic Life*, Boulder, Westview Press, 1992.

Hahn, Steven, *The Roots of Southern Populism: Yeomen Farmers and the Transformation of the Georgia Upcountry, 1850-1890*, New York, Oxford University Press, 1983.

Hamilton, Alexander, Madison, James, and Jay, John, *The Federalist: A Collection of Essays Written in Favor of the New Constitution as Agreed Upon by the Federal Convention, September 17, 1787,* Reprinted from the original text under the editorial supervision of Henry B. Dawson. Essays written by Alexander Hamilton, James Madison and John Jay under pseudonym of "Publius".

Harnack, Adolf von, *What is Christianity? Lectures Delivered in the University of Berlin During the Winter-term, 1899-1900*, 2d ed., rev. New York, G. P. Putnam's Sons, London, Williams and Norgate, 1901.

Hart, Albert Bushnell, *The Southern South*, New York, London, D. Appleton and Company, 1910.

Hill, Stuart, *Democratic Values and Technological Choices*, Stanford, Calif., Stanford University Press, 1992.

Hobbes, Thomas, *Leviathan*, London, J.M. Dent & Sons, Ltd., New York, E.P. Dutton & Co. [n.d.].

Hunt, E. K., *History of Economic Thought: A Critical Perspective,* Belmont, Calif., Wadsworth Pub. Co., 1979.

Kaufman, Gordon D., *The Theological Imagination: Constructing The Concept of God.* 1st ed., Philadelphia, Westminster Press, 1981.

Kelley, Harold H., and Thibaut, John W., *Interpersonal Relations: A Theory of Interdependence,* New York, Wiley, 1978.

Key, V. O. (Valdimer Orlando), with the assistance of Alexander Heard, *Southern Politics In State and Nation,*, New York, A. A. Knopf, 1949.

Keynes, John Maynard,. The General Theory of Employment, Interest and Money, New York, Harcourt, Brace, 1935.

Kindleberger, Charles Poor, World Economic Primacy: 1500-1910, New York, Oxford University Press, 1996.

Landes, David S., The Wealth and Poverty of Nations: Why Some Are So Rich and Some So Poor,1st ed., New York, W.W. Norton, 1998.

Lazonick, William, Organization and Technology in Capitalist Development, Aldershot, Hants, England, Brookfield, Vt., Edward Elgar, 1992.

Leakey, Richard E., and Lewin, Roger, Origins Reconsidered: In Search of What Makes Us Human, New York, Doubleday, 1992.

Lewin, Roger, The Origin of Modern Humans, New York, Scientific American Library, Distributed by W. H. Freeman, 1993.

Locke, John, The Second Treatise of Government (An Essay Concerning the True Original, Extent and End of Civil Government), and A Letter Concerning Toleration, edited by Charles L. Sherman, New York, Irvington, 1979.

Mackie, J. L. (John Leslie), Ethics: Inventing Right and Wrong, New York, Penguin, 1977.

Macpherson, C. B. (Crawford Brough), The Political Theory of Possessive Individualism:Hobbes to Locke, Oxford, Clarendon Press, 1962.

Marshall, Alfred, Elements of Economics of Industry, Being The First Volume of Elements of Economics, London and New York, Macmillan and Co., 1892.

McAdams, Robert McCormick, Paths of Fire: An Anthropologist's Inquiry Into Western Technology, Princeton, N.J., Princeton University Press, 1996.

McDonald, Forrest, Novus Ordo Seclorum: The Intellectual Origins of the Constitution, Lawrence, Kan., University Press of Kansas, 1985.

McMath, Robert C.,Populist Vanguard: A History of the Southern Farmers' Alliance, New York, Norton, 1975.

Merrill, Jensen, The Making of the American Constitution, D. Van Nostrand Co.Inc., Princeton, N.J., 1964.

Meyers, Marvin, The Mind of the Founder: Ssources of the Political Thought of James Madison, Hanover, N.H., Published for Brandeis University Press by University Press of New England, 1981.

Miles, Jack, God: A Biography, 1st ed., New York, Alfred A. Knopf, 1995.

Mill, John Stuart, Utilitarianism, Liberty, and Representative Government, Hackett Publishing Company, Inc., 1996 .

Mokyr, Joel, The Lever of Riches: Technological Creativity and Economic Progress, New York, Oxford University Press, 1990.

Morreall, John, Taking Laughter Seriously, Albany, State University of New York, 1983.

Morroni, Mario, Production Process and Technical Change, Cambridge, England, New York, Cambridge University Press, 1992.

Mowery, David C., and Rosenberg, Nathan, Paths of Innovation: Technological Change in 20th-Century America, Cambridge, New York, Cambridge University Press, 1998.

Nathans, Sydney, The Quest for Progress: The Way We Lived in North Carolina: 1870-1920, Chapel Hill, University of North Carolina Press, 1983.

Niebuhr, Reinhold, The Irony of American History, New York, Scribner, 1952.

Newby, I. A. (Idus A.), Plain Folk In The New South: Social Change and Cultural Persistence, 1880-1915, Baton Rouge, Louisiana State University Press, 1989.

Noblin, Stuart, Leonidas LaFayette Polk: A Study in Agrarian Leadership, Chapel Hill, University of North Carolina Press, 1949.

Olsen, Otto, Reconstruction and Redemtion in the South, Baton Rouge, Louisiana State University Press, 1980.

Palmer, Bruce, Man Over Money: The Southern Populist Critique of American Capitalism, Chapel Hill,University of North Carolina Press, 1980.

Pasinetti, Luigi L., Structural Change and Economic Growth: A Theoretical Essay on the Dynamics of the Wealth of Nations, Cambridge, England, New York, Cambridge University Press, 1981.

Penrose, Roger, The Emperor's New Mind: Concerning Computers, Minds, and the Laws of Physics, Oxford, New York, Oxford University Press, 1989.

Perman, Michael, *The Road to Redemption: Southern Politics, 1869-1879*, Chapel Hill, University of North Carolina Press, 1984.

Peterson, Merrill D., *The Jefferson Image In The American Mind*, New York, Oxford University Press, 1960.

Rakove, Jack N., *Declaring Rights : A Brief History With Documents*, Boston, Bedford Books, 1998.

Rawls, John, *A Theory of Justice*, Cambridge, Mass., Belknap Press of Harvard University Press, 1971.

Reiman, Jeffrey H., *Justice and Modern Moral Philosophy*, New Haven, Yale University Press, 1990.

Robinson, Joan, *Economic Philosophy*, Chicago, Aldine Pub. Co., 1962.

Rogers, Everett M., *Diffusion of Innovations*, 3rd ed., New York, Free Press, 1983.

Rosenberg, Nathan, *Inside The Black Box: Technology and Economics*, Cambridge, Cambridgeshire, New York, Cambridge University Press, 1982.

Saviotti, Paolo, *Technological Evolution, Variety, and the Economy*, Cheltenham, UK, Brookfield, Vt., E. Elgar, 1996.

Schumpeter, Joseph Alois, *The Theory of Economic Development: An Inquiry Into Profits, Capital, Credit, Interest, and the Business Cycle*, Cambridge, Mass., Harvard University Press, 1934.

Schwartz, Michael, *Radical Protest and Social Structure: The Southern Farmers' Alliance and Cotton Tenancy, 1880-1890*, New York, Academic Press, 1976.

Schweikart, Larry, *Banking In The American South From The Age Of Jackson To Reconstruction*, Baton Rouge, Louisiana State University Press, 1987.

Sen, Amartya Kumar, *Collective Choice and Social Welfare*, Amsterdam, New York, North-Holland Publishing Company, 1979.

Sheehan, Thomas, *The First Coming: How The Kingdom of God Became Christianity*, 1st ed., New York, Random House, 1986.

Sloan, Douglas, *Insight-Imagination: The Emancipation of Thought and The Modern World*, Westport, Conn., Greenwood Press, 1983.

Smith, Adam, <u>An Inquiry Into the Nature and Causes of the Wealth of Nations,</u> Oxford, Clarendon Press, 1976.

Sraffa, Piero, <u>Production of Commodities by Means of Commodities: Prelude to a Critique of Economic Theory</u>, Cambridge, Eng., University Press, 1960.

Thibaut, John W., and Kelley, John, <u>The Social Psychology of Groups,</u> New York, Wiley, 1959.

Tillich, Paul, <u>A History of Christian Thought: From Is Judaic and Hellenistic Origins to Existentialism</u>, New York, Simon and Schuster, 1972.

Tocqueville, Alexis de, <u>Democracy in America</u>. The Henry Reeve Text as rev. by Francis Bowen, now further corr. and edited with a historical essay, editorial notes, and bibliographies by Phillips Bradley. New York, Vintage Books, 1954.

Tuck, Richard, <u>Natural Rights Theories: Their Origins and Development</u>, Cambridge, Eng., New York, Cambridge University Press, 1979.

Tullos, Allen, <u>Habits of Industry: White Culture and the Transformation of the Carolina Piedmont</u>, Chapel Hill, University of North Carolina Press, 1989.

Thünen, Johann Heinrich von, <u>Isolated State: An English Edition of Der Isolierte Staat,</u> 1st ed., Oxford, New York, Pergamon Press, 1966.

Vass, Laurie Thomas, The Restoration of the American Natural Rights Republic: Correcting the Consequences of the Republican Party Abdication of Natural Rights and Individual Freedom, 3rd Edition, Raleigh, GABBY Press, 2017.

Wilson, A. N., <u>Paul: The Mind of the Apostle</u>, 1st American ed., New York, W.W. Norton & Co., 1997.

Wood, Gordon S., <u>The Creation of the American Republic: 1776-1787</u>, Chapel Hill, Published for the Institute of Early American History and Culture at Williamsburg, Va., by the University of North Carolina Press, 1969.

Wood, Phillip J., <u>Southern Capitalism: The Political Economy of North Carolina, 1880-1980</u>, Durham, N.C., Duke University Press, 1986.

Woodward, C. Vann, (Comer Vann), <u>Origins of The New South, 1877-1913,</u> 1st pbk. ed., Baton Rouge, LA., Louisiana State University Press, 1951.

Wright, Gavin, <u>Old South, New South : Revolutions in the Southern Economy Since the Civil War,</u> New York, Basic Books, 1986.

Young, J. Z., (John Zachary), <u>Philosophy and the Brain,</u> New York, Oxford University Press, 1987.

Zuckert, Michael P., <u>The Natural Rights Republic: Studies in the Foundation of the American Political Tradition,</u> Rev. ed., Notre Dame, IN., University of Notre Dame Press, 1996.

www.ingramcontent.com/pod-product-compliance
Lightning Source LLC
Chambersburg PA
CBHW052028290426
44112CB00014B/2430